David Runcorn is or has been an accordionist, vicar, fast bowler and hermit. Latterly a teacher of Spirituality and Director of Pastoral Studies at Trinity College, Bristol, he is currently the Director of Ministry Development in the Diocese of Lichfield. He is the author of several books, including *Space for God*, *Touch Wood*, *Choice, Desire and the Will of God* and *Spirituality Workbook*, and of some noted Grove publications: *Silence*, *Holiness* and *The Creation of Adam*.

To Jackie,
whose word I believed

RUMOURS OF LIFE

Transforming Wounded People

David Runcorn

First published in Great Britain in 1996 by Darton, Longman and Todd Ltd as
Rumours of Life: Reflections on Resurrection Appearances.

This revised edition published in Great Britain in 2006

Society for Promoting Christian Knowledge
36 Causton Street
London SW1P 4ST

The author and publisher have made every effort to ensure that the external website
and email addresses included in this book are correct and up to date at the time of
going to press. The author and publisher are not responsible for the content, quality
or continuing accessibility of the sites.

Every effort has been made to acknowledge fully the sources of material reproduced
in this book. The publisher apologizes for any omissions that may remain and, if
notified, will ensure that full acknowledgements are made in a subsequent edition.

British Library Cataloguing-in-Publication Data
A catalogue record for this book is available from the British Library.

ISBN-13: 978–0–281–05869–3
ISBN-10: 0–281–05869–5

10 9 8 7 6 5 4 3 2 1

Typeset by Kenneth Burnley, Wirral, Cheshire
Printed in Great Britain by Bookmarque Ltd, Croydon, Surrey

Contents

Contents

Preface to the new edition

The first version of this book grew out of life in the lively and always thoughtful congregation of St Stephen's Church, West London, where I was their vicar. It travelled with me to Bristol where, at Trinity Theological College, I was involved in the training and formation of men and women preparing for all kinds of ministry in the wider Church.

It now emerges in a fully revised and updated edition, with a new introduction. And I am working as Director of Ministry Development in the large, diverse diocese of Lichfield in the West Midlands.

What these three contexts share is the challenge of exploring how people and communities are enabled to enter the transforming life of the Christian gospel. The task has never felt more pressing and the themes of this book never more relevant.

I gratefully acknowledge my personal debt to these three very contrasting communities, for the different ways in which they have made real to me what it means to follow Jesus into the gift of his life.

My thanks to Alison Barr, Senior Editor at SPCK, for guiding this book into a re-birth.

Lastly, my love and thanks to my wife Jackie and my two boys, Josh and Simeon – joyful travel companions throughout. A writer is not always easy company in a family. When the first edition of this book appeared, Jackie gave me a copy with the title subtly adapted to *Rumours of Wife*!

It is a rumour I am grateful to confirm.

Introduction

In search of words that raise the dead

———◆———

What gives you hope in a world like ours?

I am not asking if you are optimistic. I mean something much deeper than a capacity to look on the bright side, laugh at problems, smile in adversity or to 'talk up' the positives in the face of disaster. That is partly a matter of temperament. I envy such people (though at other times I confess I badly want to damage them!). A naturally 'sunny' disposition is a genuine gift to have around. But in a culture so chronically anxious and allergic to pain, this may so easily be a way of denying and avoiding things we really need to be facing.

To be hopeful is to meet life from a very different place. It involves a tough engagement with life as it really is. To hope means being utterly realistic about what we are facing. And yet somewhere deep within, an improbable belief takes hold. Vulnerable but tenacious, it won't let us go and we cannot quite shake it off either. It is basically an improbable conviction that all this is part of another story entirely, yet to be revealed. A transformation promised. An unexpected destiny barely glimpsed yet compelling. And all the while the evidence of our eyes points firmly to the contrary.

So what is your hope? Where does it come from? These are, after all, profoundly unsettling times to be living in. The most familiar patterns can no longer be relied on. All is change. How do you hope when so much is uncertain? Two people were discussing this on the radio. 'The future isn't what it used to be,' says one. 'No,' says the other, 'and the past isn't getting any better either.'

Bishop Lesslie Newbigin was one of the great visionary leaders and teachers of the international Church in the last hundred years. Whenever he was asked what gave him hope he would reply that there was only one answer – 'that God raised Jesus Christ from the dead'.

This book explores the challenge of that startling answer by looking at the stories of the first disciples meeting the risen Jesus in the weeks after the first Easter Day.

Living in between

For a long while my approach to Christian faith was driven by a certain expectation of what resurrection life was meant to be like. In 'real' resurrection life, the air was always clear, faith was certain, bold and exciting. Jesus was unmistakably real and near. Christian testimony was positive and 'over-coming'. The volume control of this faith was always set on 'loud'. Life was peppered with exclamation marks.

I tried very hard and I believe the desire to please God does please him. But this approach often left me feeling exhausted and inadequate. And there was a deeper issue. Like the preacher who would write in the margin of his sermon notes, 'Shout loud here, argument weak', my understanding and actual experience of resurrection were not in a good relationship. In fact they were not on speaking terms at times. I was throwing myself passionately after an elusive experience, while the truth was actually something quite different. My own life of faith was actually much more contradictory (as it was for many of my friends as well). Oh, I knew the love of Christ at work in my life. But there were times when I also felt very lost and confused, times when risen life seemed very far away.

I was trapped in an approach to faith that vigorously proclaimed new life and urged me to forsake the old, but which was not very good at telling me how to get from one to the other. As most of us spend our lives in 'in-between' places, this was not very helpful.

The resurrection stories are 'in-between stories' that have much to teach about how faith and hope are formed among lost and wounded people.

There can be a misplaced zeal in believing that requires the experience to be clearer and more definite than it actually is. A missionary Church, facing decline, seeking to persuade the surrounding post-Christian world, feels this pressure keenly. This must be convincing and exciting. Nothing less will do. (So it is hard to even admit this without feeling that such faith is lacking something.) But I recall the wisdom of a woman, newly drawn to faith, who was put under great pressure in a Christian prayer group because the other members suspected she had not had the 'real thing' yet:

> Only men could speak about birth as if it were a quick thing, with an immediate change of 'before' and 'after'. Any woman knows that birth is long and slow, very painful and very messy. You expose the most embarrassing parts of yourself and are so vulnerable that you are past caring. If that is what real birth is like, then why should spiritual birth be any different?[1]

Approaching resurrection

You can't spend long trying to understand the resurrection without discovering that you are sitting astride one of the traditional theological fault-lines in the Christian faith. This is not surprising as the very heart of our faith is revealed there. The empty tomb is not simply there to be 'explained' as if establishing the *facts* were all that is needed. When your belief in the resurrection is questioned, the natural response is to go on the defensive and argue back. That is not wrong of course. The willingness and ability to debate issues of faith has never been more important. But the process easily distorts the nature of faith. Easter becomes an argument to be won rather than a mystery to be entered.

Another related tendency is to start with 'resurrection' as the general idea and to dip into the resurrection stories to illustrate the more general point that is being made. This distorts the significance of these encounters. They are not there to confirm our theories.

That is why I so love this unexpected cluster of stories on the far side of the grave. These are not careful doctrinal statements of faith: we must look elsewhere for those.[2] Raw shock, fear and astonishment are the most common features of these encounters. That first Christian community has simply shared its stories of journey into new life. Their slowness, turmoil and unbelief are recorded without excuse or justification.

It is very significant that the ancient yearly cycle of Christian worship and teaching sets apart a period for special focus on the resurrection that is as long as the more familiar season of Lent. Risen life needs every bit as much attention, disciplined reflection and prayerful living as penitence and sin. In practice it receives considerably less.

In revisiting these stories to prepare the new edition of this book, I have felt their relevance to our present age with renewed force. We need these stories. They are pastoral and missionary stories for uncertain times. The gift of these brief, enigmatic and personal encounters is to help us to understand this mysterious journey into new birth – of conversion to Christ and life in the transforming gift of his love.

To read these stories requires us to struggle with their sheer strangeness. Tom Wright's comprehensive study of resurrection contains a long chapter in which the word 'strangeness' appears repeatedly.[3] And it is not our job to tidy anything of this up by 'explaining' it.

Christian faith in our land is a matter of increasing irrelevance. In response to this, the Church is urgently seeking initiatives and resources by which to challenge and capture the imagination of this generation in new ways. Many of these resources are excellent and are having an impact. But that very pressure means that the message itself is easily oversimplified or comes pre-packaged. Its relevance to us and our needs is made central. The sheer quirkiness and strangeness of Christian believing is lost. The process has been called the 'McDonaldization of the gospel'. This is consumerist and needs resisting passionately. These stories offer a very different wisdom on how people and communities journey and grow towards transformation and faith.

There is a saving *irrelevance* about these encounters and how they are offered to us. This is precisely what makes these stories good news. They simply don't buy in to our sense of what we need – our preoccupations and consumer appetites. They have nothing to offer us at all on those terms.

In fact a publisher today would surely send all these stories back to the authors for extensive revision. After all, they miss out crucial information. They don't always agree with each other on facts. They spend time on insignificant details. They leave important questions unanswered. And many of the stories are just left unfinished and their message unclear.

There is also a strange lack of urgency running through all this Easter period. Even Jesus seems to come and go without obvious concern for any particular task or job to do. By the standards of our driven world, there seems no concern for a product, for goal setting or results. There is virtually no dramatic build-up to his great commission and his ascension to heaven. In fact, at the moment of commissioning on the mountain we read that when they saw him they worshipped, 'but some doubted' (Matthew 28.17, and see Chapter 8).

On this evidence, risen life is not for those who are ready to receive it. The only people in the Gospels to receive the resurrection were all totally and utterly *un*ready. Christ comes to such people gently and with infinite care. He knows what his transforming life must ask of them. Rather than immediately healing and transforming, the resurrection of Jesus must bring a deeper wound of its own. It must cut through all our ways of understanding, hoping and living. It will overthrow all our carefully guarded securities.

Our hope is this – that God raised Jesus from the dead. And Jesus comes to us as he did to those first disciples, wherever he must find us, taking whatever time it needs. He will minister among us until his word and gift can be received. He will guide us through what has been rightly described as the 'harrowing operation of conversion'.[4]

And so to this vulnerable and fallen world, now gloriously 'wounded by Grace',[5] the resurrection is not announced with deafening thunder, brilliant skies or blinding certainties and urgent mission, but by a rumour – a rumour of life.

'Christ is risen.'

1

A door has cracked open

The empty tomb

When it was evening, there came a rich man from Arimathea, named Joseph, who was also a disciple of Jesus. He went to Pilate and asked for the body of Jesus; then Pilate ordered it to be given to him. So Joseph took the body and wrapped it in a clean linen cloth and laid it in his own new tomb, which he had hewn in the rock. He then rolled a great stone to the door of the tomb and went away.

(Matthew 27.57–60)

Most stories end at this point. But this is where the Christian faith begins.

Something happened in the night.

What God chooses to reveal or keep secret is always a puzzle. A tomb left empty, stone rolled away, waiting for someone to discover it, is a puzzling way to launch a new world.

God has acted in the dark, when no one is around. No cameras were there to capture this unique and unrepeatable event. There were no press releases; no witnesses to question.

Long before daybreak and the arrival of any human beings, God raised the dead and opened the tomb for all to see what he had done.

Christian teaching about the resurrection of Jesus has always insisted that the tomb was empty. Even while differing on other details, all four Gospels agree on this fact. The tomb itself was very public knowledge. It was owned by a prominent member of Jerusalem high society, Joseph of Arimathea (Matthew 27.57–60). His request to Pilate for the body was also very public – and in the circumstances courageous, even scandalous. He was offering to give his own tomb to a man condemned for blasphemy and executed as a common criminal. We know that the tomb was close to the place of crucifixion and that it was located in a private garden (John 19.41–42). Joseph was assisted in the burial by Nicodemus, another prominent religious leader (John 19.39). Several witnesses watched them place the body of Jesus in the tomb and seal it (Matthew 27.61; Luke 23.55).

Short of putting a map and directions to the tomb into their accounts, the Gospels, taken together, could hardly have been more specific.

In the small and intense world of Jerusalem society, the location of that unusual tomb would have been notoriously well known.

This was the tomb that was found empty, early on Easter morning. The stone was rolled away. The body of Jesus was gone. There were angels around and the grave-clothes had even been neatly folded.

Are you surprised?

Absurd belief

Unless we feel the shock and even absurdity of this story, we have not understood it. The dead don't rise. It doesn't happen. But we know this story too well. We come to Easter morning like people reading a novel who have already read the last chapter and know how it all ends. The tomb has lost its power to surprise us.

But it overwhelmed the first Christian communities. 'The New Testament breathes an air of astonishment,' says Philip Seddon, 'the air of the first liberated people of creation, travellers emerging from a dark night into the brilliance of a long-awaited day, spellbound by God's inexpressible gift of himself.'[1]

The Christian Church has coped in different ways with the sheer strangeness of its own story at this point. For some, the idea of a dead body physically rising is simply not credible in a modern scientific world. The story is therefore not to be read as actual history. Its meaning is reinterpreted for its 'spiritual' significance.

Those wanting to defend these accounts as reliable history are often prone to do so in an aggressively factual way, as if there is a logical case to be made. The end result is the same. We end up with an Easter message that is credible and believable on our own terms.

But that first Easter was completely *un*believable.

None of the disciples came to believe in the resurrection of Jesus on the evidence of the tomb alone. Quite the reverse: it was a further tragedy. No one was expecting it.

They were still traumatized by the events of the weekend only to be plunged into further grief and confusion by what they found. They appeared too dazed and helpless even to search the site or alert the authorities. That is what makes the abrupt (original) ending of Mark's Gospel seem so believable. The impression he gives is that the ministry of angels only made things worse. Nothing could calm their terror. 'So they went out and fled from the tomb, for terror and amazement had seized them; and they said nothing to anyone, for they were afraid' (Mark 16.8).

Coming to the tomb

An empty tomb is a mysterious, dramatic place. Like the irresistible attraction of exploring caves in the cliffs on holiday, I find myself wanting to go in and explore this one. And that is precisely what we are meant to feel. The journey to the tomb is one we all have to make. It is there for us to discover too. The tomb was not opened to let Jesus out. It was opened to let us in.

An earlier form of the Communion Service spoke of God who '*revealed* the resurrection' by raising Jesus to new life.[2] The phrase always struck me as significant. It implied that the resurrection itself was never in doubt. God cannot die. But the surprise and gift of Easter is that this resurrection is for us too. Jesus has been raised in our flesh and blood. It is our death that has been defeated.

There is a need to recover the empty tomb as a place of spiritual pilgrimage and imaginative prayer. Some churches use their Communion table for this. Late on Good Friday the table becomes a tomb, surrounded in sacking, with an opening at the front. A large round 'stone' (made of card or papier mâché) is placed across the entrance. There may be a special service of lament, recalling the burial of Jesus.

On Easter Sunday the children roll the stone away and look carefully to see if there is anyone inside. All they find are some folded sheets. What has happened? Curiosity and faith are awakened in the recovery of playful, childlike wonder.

Death of death

There are those who claim that the empty tomb is itself irrelevant to the Easter message and that attempts to make it a basis for faith are misguided. But its place at the centre of the Easter story is vital. Not because it proves anything: it doesn't. It is significant for what it points to.

First, the empty tomb reveals an act of God. The resurrection is first and foremost something that happened to Jesus rather than something that happened to the disciples. Attempts to reinterpret the Easter story invariably place the emphasis on the latter. But it is highly questionable whether the disciples would have arrived at the idea of resurrection on their own. 'The disciples were prepared neither psychologically nor theologically for the idea of resurrection of a crucified messiah, and the fact that they arrived at this idea so early and confidently needs an explanation.'[3]

Second, the empty tomb witnesses to the physical resurrection of Jesus from the dead. This traditional belief has come in for heavy criticism from some modern interpreters. Some claim that the stories of an empty tomb were invented later to strengthen the Church's resurrection message.

This raises more problems than it answers. For one thing, it is hardly likely that a story written later would have included such specific, historical details. There would have been no point in including details that could be easily checked – not least the inclusion of a highly respected leader of Jewish society who was not known (until that point) to be a follower of Jesus.

No one inventing the story would have chosen women as the first witnesses either (see Chapter 5). The accounts do not read like later inventions. No attempt has been made to smooth out confusing differences in detail between the Gospels. They have all the vividness and clumsiness of eye-witness accounts. Information later readers might think essential is omitted (such as the content of much of Jesus' teaching) and apparently irrelevant details are recorded (such as the folded grave-clothes in the tomb).

Third, the empty tomb connects the resurrection with the cross. The one who has risen is the one who died. There is no room here for theories suggesting that the resurrection appearances involved some kind of substitution or mistaken identity. Moreover, the witness of the tomb is confirmed by the wounds of crucifixion upon the risen Jesus. It is by those same wounds that the disciples fully recognized him (John 20.20, and see Chapter 7).

Finally, the empty tomb separates Christian faith from 'spiritualizing' theories of resurrection and ideas of the immortality of the soul. This is the belief that the human spirit is in some way 'naturally' eternal and continues life beyond physical death. Resurrection is the release of my spirit or soul into new life, 'liberated' from the constraints of my mortal body. Nowhere does the Bible teach this. On the contrary, the Christian hope of salvation is for the transformation of the body as well as spirit.[4]

> The Christian resurrection claim is an *empirical* claim: it entails the life after death of *living bodies* (although of a transformed sort) that can be seen and touched. The resurrection does not mean that, much to our pleasant surprise, we human beings turn out to have an indestructible aspect that survives death. It means rather that death has been defeated by a miraculous and decisive intervention by God.[5]

The open door

In Tom Stoppard's play *Arcadia*, Valentine explains, with growing excitement, the way that Chaos theory has thrown the settled world of science into confusion. It has overturned the old order based on the binding predictability of Newtonian physics. The changes it is bringing are uncertain. But it promises, for Valentine, a revolution that is full of new life and possibilities. It involves a radical transformation in the way that the world and all within it is understood. The change is so complete that it feels as if life itself is starting all over again. On the threshold of this new age he rejoices in language of exhilarating faith.

> It makes me so happy. To be at the beginning again, knowing almost nothing. The future is disorder. A door like this has cracked open five or six times since we got up on our hind legs. It's the best possible time to be alive, when almost everything you thought you knew is wrong.[6]

His words would not have been out of place before the discovery of the empty tomb.

Risen indeed

Throughout the history of the Church the empty tomb has stood as a silent inspiration to Christians facing the most extreme persecution and suffering. The belief that death itself has been defeated makes faith and hope possible in otherwise impossible circumstances.

As a student in Moscow at the height of state persecution of Christians, Michael Bourdeaux attended the Easter celebration at an Orthodox church. What he experienced there changed his life. He stood in the darkness and listened to the procession approaching the church chanting the Easter liturgy. 'They have taken away my Lord and I do not know where they have laid him.' 'Whom seek ye?' 'The body of Jesus.' 'Why seek ye the living among the dead? He is not here. He is risen – *Khristos voskrese!*' The Paschal Candle was lit in the darkness.

In less than a minute five thousand individual flames united in one faith. Each candle lit up a face behind. That face bore the deep lines of sorrow, of personal tragedy. Yet, as it was illuminated, the suffering turned to joy, to the certain knowledge of the reality of the risen Lord.

Often since that Easter midnight I reflect how that single five minutes of experience taught me the certainty of the resurrection in a way that reading a hundred theological books had not quite managed to do. 'How could they be so sure?' I asked myself. The answer always came back: they have trodden the way of the cross to the hill of Calvary. Their suffering under Stalin stripped them of every material advantage and reward; they were imprisoned; dear ones died in every family.

They do not debate the resurrection: they have experienced its reality in their own lives. They have not preserved the faith in hostile surroundings; it has preserved them. Their joy is truly a glimpse through the curtain which divides us from heaven.[7]

When Archbishop Janani Luwum was murdered in Uganda for his opposition to the brutal reign of President Idi Amin, his body was not released to his family and church for burial, and gatherings were banned. But a grave had already been dug in the grounds of the cathedral and thousands of people gathered there.

> Our eyes fell on the empty grave, a gaping hole in the earth. The words of the angel to the two women seeking Jesus's body flashed into our minds. 'Why do you see the living among the dead?' Namirembe Hill resounded with the song that the balokole ('the saved ones') have taken as their own:
>
> > Glory, glory, hallelujah,
> > Glory, glory to the Lamb!
> > Oh, the cleansing blood has reached me,
> > Glory, glory to the Lamb.
>
> We came away healed by the revelation of the empty grave.[8]

Upside-down believing

I once had a meeting with a couple who wanted a church wedding. As they had no Christian background I started by telling them about Jesus and spoke of the cross and resurrection. They were already looking bored. Then I said, 'Of course, if he rose from the dead then he's around now – he's here with us.' They reacted immediately. The groom only just resisted the urge to check if anyone was behind the sofa. The bride went pale and admitted, 'It sounds a bit spooky.'

The incident shook me too. I had not expected their surprise. I realized that I had ceased to speak of the resurrection with any sense of wonder. This is the peril of overfamiliarity. The truth is that 'the resurrection is not just a unique and improbable event but an intellectual scandal. It is the sort of event that conflicts so radically with so many well-established scientific laws that any attempt to revise them in such a way as to allow for resurrection would vitiate them.'[9]

We should not be surprised if *any* age finds the idea of resurrection difficult or unacceptable. The world of the first disciples found it just as difficult.

The Gospels were not written to confirm any prevailing view of the world, but to challenge and transform it: 'these [words] are written so that you may come to believe that Jesus is the Messiah, the Son of God, and that through believing you may have life in his name' (John 20.31).

In any age, believing the resurrection of Jesus requires what Charles Handy calls 'upside-down thinking'. He was writing about those times in history when an event or series of events so contradicts what has gone before that it throws old ways of thinking and understanding into chaos. It requires new and *un*reasonable ways of thinking and acting to respond to it, '*even if both thinkers and thoughts appear absurd at first sight*' (my italics).[10]

Handy believes that Western civilization is in the midst of just such a time of critical change and that the outcome is not at all certain. If he is right then Christian faith is well equipped to live within such a world. For the resurrection is completely unreasonable. God has broken all the rules. The empty tomb is the ultimate act of what Handy calls '*discon-tinuous change*'. Resurrection life requires upside-down thinking, and the closer to the truth we get, the more we will also feel the absurdity of what we believe.

Among the dead

I caught this truth unexpectedly while leading a Quiet Day for clergy at a retreat house in Essex. It was shortly after Easter and I decided to speak on the resurrection stories. After the first address I encouraged the group to spend time alone imagining themselves among the first disciples on Easter Day. The weather was warm and most people went into the large garden at the back of the building.

Only a little later did I realize that the garden was the resting place for early generations of Quaker families. I looked out on to a rather unkempt lawn, a battered old chil-dren's climbing frame on one side and clergy sitting and lying among the gravestones contemplating resurrection.

> In the morning,
> long after day break,
> we came to the garden
> and found a graveyard.
> No one had rolled
> away the stones.
>
> And standing forlorn
> among the tombs
> a child's climbing frame

A door has cracked open

rusted,
abandoned,
like a badly misjudged gift,
for who comes to play
at the mouth of the grave,
and do the dead need
recreation?

But *someone's* weight
had bent those rungs.
Beside the stones we wondered.

There in the garden
which is a graveyard
and was a playground
began
(and not for the first time)
a rumour of angels
while somewhere near,
discreet,
not wishing to offend,
their laughter all above
our ears,
they played away that
long hot day,
just killing time
(which is their work)
and wondered that we sat
    among the dead.[11]

2

Loving the space between

The risen absence of Jesus

⇒►○◄⇐

Very early on the first day of the week, when the sun had risen,
they went to the tomb. They had been saying to one another,
'Who will roll away the stone for us from the entrance to the
tomb?' When they looked up, they saw that the stone, which
was very large, had already been rolled back. As they entered
the tomb, they saw a young man, dressed in a white robe, sitting
on the right side; and they were alarmed. But he said to them,
'Do not be alarmed; you are looking for Jesus of Nazareth, who
was crucified. He has been raised; he is not here. Look, there is
the place they laid him.'

(Mark 16.2–7)

The first experience of resurrection for the disciples was not
presence but absence. Jesus was gone and they didn't know
where. While angels kept telling them what good news it
was, the situation left them in turmoil.

According to Mark's Gospel the women found it all so
terrifying that they fled from the tomb in fear and didn't tell
anyone what they had seen (16.8).

In fact, in the 40 days that followed, Jesus seems to have

been much more absent than present. We have records of up to eight appearances by Jesus (though it is impossible to be precise) and many of the encounters described were quite brief. This means that the disciples had a great deal of time between meetings with Jesus. The evidence of the resurrection stories is that Jesus gives his disciples a lot of space.

It is very curious that Jesus seems to spend so *little* time with his disciples. At such a critical time of preparation for the new age of the Church we might suppose that he would want to pack every risen day with training courses, retreats, leadership training, workshops on healing and counselling. Instead all we have is a handful of unpredictable and enigmatic encounters with individuals or groups of disciples.

While endless sermons and books are written on the resurrection *presence* of Jesus, his risen *absence* is almost totally ignored. The angels were quite clear – he is risen, he is *not* here. The risen Jesus does not automatically mean the present Jesus.

Divine absence

We start with a basic problem. A great deal of Christian believing has no positive understanding of God's absence at all. I don't mean that God is truly absent. I am thinking of those times when he seems to withdraw his presence and we cannot find him. He is not where we expected him to be. Then we tend to believe that it must be because we have done something wrong. We accuse ourselves. I am not praying enough. I have sinned. God doesn't love me any more. He is teaching me a lesson. After all, hasn't he promised never to leave us?

I once bumped into a friend in a Christian bookshop. He was buying up all the books he could find on such subjects as 'Restoring your spiritual passion' and 'Victorious Christian living'. As we talked it was clear he was in turmoil. A previously lively faith had gone totally dry on him. He was desperately looking for a way of recovering the old feeling. God seemed so far away. He was absent where he had always been present. I sat there listening, with the uncomfortable feeling that my friend had just wasted his money. The grace God was giving him was his absence, not his presence. And if that was where God wanted him then no amount of spiritual reading would change that. He must learn to wait in the dark and emptiness.

Part of my friend's pain was that nothing in his Christian life had prepared him for an absence of God that wasn't either the failure of faith or the death of it.

Our problem is that we have neglected those parts of Christian teaching down the centuries that have understood and even stressed the importance of divine absence, of darkness, desert and emptiness in the Christian experience. One classic book on prayer from the Russian Orthodox tradition actually begins with a whole chapter on the absence of God. It affirms there are times when God withdraws his presence out of love and a desire to protect us. This is necessary because every meeting with God is a moment of judgement for us. God is truth, holiness, power. We cannot seek his presence lightly. His love is like a consuming fire for us. So the author's advice is to be thankful to God 'that he does not always present himself to us when we wish to meet him, because we might not be able to endure such a meeting'.[1]

The tyranny of presence

There can be a misplaced loyalty to the *presence* of Christ which can be exhausting and oppressive. Unless the presence of God is balanced by a positive understanding of his absence, then our experience may become exhausting and even destructive. Some years ago I came to a personal crisis in my life. At rock bottom and close to a breakdown, I was near to giving up ministry and faith. I was very grateful for those friends who knew and supported me. But I remember how often I heard people praying for God's presence to be real to me. I didn't know how to tell them that that was exactly what I *didn't* want. His presence had become a total burden. I wanted his absence. I wanted space.

But the midst of enthusiastic Christian fellowship is not the place you can say that sort of thing (and especially not if you are a vicar!). I needed someone to pray: 'Lord, it gets a bit too much with you around at times. You can be very demanding. David needs a break. Stop trying to help. It just makes it worse. Leave him alone for a bit and give him a rest.'

A story in the novel *Zorba the Greek* spoke very clearly to me at this time and has stayed with me ever since.

I remembered one morning when I discovered a cocoon in the bark of a tree, just as the butterfly was making a hole in its case and preparing to come out. I waited a little while, but it was too long appearing and I was impatient.

I bent over it and breathed on it to warm it. I warmed it as quickly as I could and the miracle began to happen before my eyes, faster than life.

The case opened, the butterfly started slowly crawling out and I shall never forget my horror [. . .] when I saw how its wings were folded back and crumpled. The wretched butterfly tried with its whole trembling body to unfold them. Bending over it I tried to help it with my breath. In vain. It needed to be hatched out patiently and the unfolding of the wings would be a gradual process in the sun. Now it was too late. My breath had forced the butterfly to appear, all crumpled, before its time. It struggled desperately and, a few seconds later, died in the palm of my hand.[2]

The experience was hard but life-changing.

Perhaps for my own survival I took myself off to the Alps and spent two months in a cabin on my own. Up there in my amateur hermitage, I remember weeping bitterly. My experience of Christianity had been just such a hot breath, a constant forcing before its time, a suffocating presence. Christian life for me had been intensely about presence – the presence of God, of the Church, the

18

world, my friends, my work. Faith had all but died. If I was to know risen life it would have to come another way.[3]

Giving space

'Giving space' is not usually the way the Church goes about its life. Nor is it the way many Christians would describe their experience of Church! There are practical reasons for this. Most churches are facing huge pressures, and resources are stretched ever more thinly. They need everyone to be *more* committed and involved, not less. But whether out of enthusiasm or anxiety, it is perilously easy to force people to grow and respond at the pace we require rather than giving them the time and space they actually need.

Some have had religion forced on them at some earlier stage of their life. It may have been a well-intended pressure but it has left them unwilling to get too close to a God who had so violated their space, imposing his heavy presence with exhausting demands that lacked all nurture, humour and love. There is often a deep weariness of spirit in such people which is difficult to reach.

More commonly, in a post-Christian age, the need to keep distance comes from being part of a culture that is marked by reluctance to be committed to *any* community, institution or organization. The intensity of so much contemporary living and the pressures it imposes leaves many of us easily overwhelmed and instinctively keeping as safe a distance as we can.

If people are to come to trust the Christian message and belong to the community that seeks to live it, they will need a great deal of space where they can begin to tell their story and find the trust they require to open up to their deepest needs.

What some people want is the grace of God's *absence*. There are lessons of faith and awareness we only learn alone. Even God must withdraw from us.

An American priest with a very busy national speaking ministry spoke of a time when he felt God tell him to keep every morning empty for the whole month leading up to Christmas. He described his struggles day by day. As the grip of his previous lifestyle began to lessen in the silence, he came to look on his own ministry and life with new eyes. He saw that much of what he thought was 'spiritual' and important was actually his own ambition and refined show-manship. He called that whole time a process of drastic detoxification – from his own busy-ness, from his need for recognition and importance. He was being weaned off deep-seated addictions to religious activity – the obsessive-ness that we so easily confuse for the real thing.

The grace of God's absence prepared him in a new way to be a minister of his presence.

The resurrection stories understand our need for space.

Unmasking illusion

Anyone who has spent time in silent retreat will have known something of this struggle. Coming from very busy lives we need time to stop and unwind and become still. We come longing for space, but as the silence takes hold and stillness grows around us, the absence of people or things to do can become deeply unsettling. The temptation is to fill up the space. Anything will do. At such times the need to make coffee every half-hour can have an almost demonic intensity.

In the space that is God's absence, our religious games are eventually seen in all their emptiness. Our false pictures of God and ourselves are exposed for what they are. Our ploys for trying to control God are uncovered. In the Bible the place of God's absence is the wilderness. It is the place where faith is purified and where the power of false gods is broken. It is for this reason that Thomas Merton, writing of the importance of solitude, described Christian prayer as 'the unmasking of illusion'.

Pastoral ministry is never more painful than at times like that, when you know that you can offer nothing to take away the pain of a person's journey through what feels like abandonment, desolation and emptiness. You can only affirm the absence as the risen absence of Christ. To be there is not a failure but a sign of grace. There is nothing else to do but wait in the dark. A superficial comfort, a spiritual sticking-plaster, at such a time is no solution at all.

One of the most healing gifts we can offer each other in the midst of this driven, distracted world is not more and better ways of doing things. It is simply a safe 'space'. This will be somewhere we can come, reflect, talk (if we wish), listen and so seek to deepen the roots of our living and understanding. This is such a hard world in which to live at any depth and it leaves us profoundly dis-eased.

The space between

The simplest and most obvious thing that Jesus was teaching the disciples after the resurrection was how to have a living relationship with him. After all, the freedom to be absent or present with someone is what makes real friendship possible. The truth is that any relationship that is based entirely on presence quickly becomes suffocating and oppressive. This is as true of our relating to God as to each another. Walker Percy was struggling with this when he wrote, with characteristic directness: 'Christ should leave us. He is too much with us and I don't like his friends. We have no hope of recovering Christ until Christ leaves us. There is after all something worse than being God-forsaken. It is when God overstays his welcome and takes up with the wrong people.'[4]

The ability to love another is not measured by how close we can get. It is actually about the freedom to give the right space. Too close and our possessive clinging will choke all life out of our relationship. Too distant and we will simply drift apart.

In his meditation on marriage, Kahlil Gibran affirms all that unites a couple but urges, 'Let there be spaces in your togetherness. And let the winds of heaven dance between you [. . .] but let each of you be alone.'[5]

The poet Rainer Rilke says the same thing more strongly: 'I hold this to be the highest task of a bond between two people: that each should stand guard over the solitude of the other.' They are to encourage each other's solitude and their times together are 'true sharings which interrupt periods of deep isolation'.[6] This sounds a complete contradiction alongside the popular understanding of loving. Love is surely about being together, not being apart? But in another place Rilke develops this idea more fully.

> *Togetherness* between two human beings is an impossibility and, when it seems to occur, a limitation, a mutual compromise, which robs one side, or both, of their fullest freedom and development. But once the awareness is granted, that even between the closest of human beings there remains an infinite distance, then a wonderful living-alongside-each-other can spring up, when they succeed in loving the distance between, something that makes it possible for them to see each other in their wholeness and against the background of the vastness of heaven.[7]

The freedom to love

'He is *not* here.' Risen life means learning to live between the absence and presence of Christ – and to love the space between. For the risen Jesus, Jesus the Lord, is an absence that is never abandonment and a presence that is not possession.

He gives to his disciples the degree of space that makes real loving possible. And in that space we may freely learn to love him in a relationship that is as terrifying as it is glorious.

I have come to picture the absent Jesus, just out of sight of the disciples, present to all their fearful watching and waiting, quietly standing guard over their solitude.

3

Why are you weeping?

Mary at the tomb

Early on the first day of the week, while it was still dark, Mary
Magdalene came to the tomb and saw that the stone had been
removed from the tomb. So she ran and went to Simon Peter
and the other disciple, the one whom Jesus loved, and said to
them, 'They have taken the Lord out of the tomb, and we do
not know where they have laid him.' Then the disciples
returned to their homes.

But Mary stood weeping outside the tomb. As she wept, she
bent over to look into the tomb; and she saw two angels in
white, sitting where the body of Jesus had been lying, one at the
head and the other at the feet. They said to her, 'Woman, why
are you weeping?' She said to them, 'They have taken away my
Lord, and I do not know where they have laid him.' When she
had said this, she turned round and saw Jesus standing there,
but she did not know that it was Jesus. Jesus said to her,
'Woman, why are you weeping? For whom are you looking?'
Supposing him to be the gardener, she said to him, 'Sir, if you
have carried him away, tell me where you have laid him, and I
will take him away.' Jesus said to her, 'Mary!' She turned and
said to him in Hebrew, 'Rabbouni!' (which means Teacher).

(John 20.1–2, 10–16)

A woman standing by a tomb. This could be a scene from anywhere in the world.

But Mary had not come to mourn. There was still work to be done: the burial of Jesus was not complete. In that culture the burial of the dead included important rituals of anointing, and there had not been time to complete these before the start of the Sabbath. This explains the conversation recorded in Mark's Gospel where we read that Mary, in company with other women, was worried about how they were going to move the stone away from the entrance and get into the tomb (Mark 16.2–3).

Jesus was laid in a rich man's tomb, which would have been a family vault. The body would have been left in the small ante-chamber waiting for final anointing and then burial in one of the smaller vaults hollowed out of the rock face at the back of the tomb.

When the women arrived they were astonished to find that the tomb was already open – and empty. There was a burst of hectic activity. Peter and others came running to check. The body of Jesus was definitely not there. The shock and confusion are all described in a few short verses (John 20.6–7).

The story began with Mary, however, and it now returns to her. The other characters, the noise and excitement, all die away. We are left with Mary, alone outside the tomb. She is weeping.

This is a story about tears and resurrection.

The grace of tears

Mary weeps. That in itself may be enviable. For we are not a culture that quite knows what to do with tears. I mean real tears. At one level our world is happy to indulge in any emotion if the mood takes us. But to faithfully attend to those emotions as they express the truth of our deeper hurts and longings is much less easy. For many of us this means overcoming an ambivalence that is learned from our earliest years. We learn we must keep them hidden. Crying is childish. It is a weakness. It is indulgent. Weeping is a social embarrassment. Someone in tears will be led away to somewhere quiet. Though this may actually be a sensitive response at times, to the distressed person it can also feel like a subtle form of 'removal'.

We actually use the language of bodily malfunction when we talk about tears. We call it 'breaking down' or 'losing it'. We try to 'pull ourselves together' or 'get a grip on ourselves'. Time and again I have watched mourners at funerals struggling to hold back tears as if they were wrong or inappropriate. I have listened to people telling the most harrowing stories and then apologizing for their tears as if they were an indulgence. This varies greatly across cultures – but tears have never been very 'British'. They are to be kept firmly under control and so our grief is repressed.

By contrast, the culture in which the Bible was written was much more open and relaxed about emotions in

general. The people of the scriptures had no such inhibitions. Tears were accepted. They guided the faithful
through grief and struggle and renewed them in their
pilgrimage.

> May those who sow in tears
>   reap with shouts of joy.
> Those who go out weeping,
>   bearing the seed for sowing,
> shall come home with shouts of joy,
>   carrying their sheaves.
>
> (Psalm 126.5–6)

> Blessed are those . . .
>   whose hearts are set on pilgrimage.
> As they pass through the Valley of Tears
> they make there a water hole,
> and – a further blessing – early rain fills it.
>
> (Psalm 84.5–6, NJB)

Jesus even taught that grieving was a blessed gift (Matthew
5.5). In the Sermon on the Mount he pronounced a special
blessing on those who mourn. He himself is recorded as
weeping and expressing deep emotion on many occasions,
and is remembered, in the words of Isaiah, as a 'man of
sorrows'. Tears often flowed in the Gospels when people met
Jesus and experienced his love and healing. In the very
moving story of the prostitute who caused a scandal by
weeping over the feet of Jesus before drying them with

her hair, Jesus received her action as an anointing (Luke 7.36–50).

What is less well known among Christians today is the way the Church down the centuries has always given special importance to tears in the spiritual life. The presence of tears was reverenced as a mark of grace. They were seen as a sign of God's Spirit at work in the deep places of a Christian's life. They released the believer to fresh repentance and renewed self-offering. The gift of tears was to be sought from God.

In the early centuries of the Church, the writings of the great spiritual teachers, such as Gregory Nazianzen, Ephraim the Syrian, John Climacus and Symeon the New Theologian, all included long discussions on the importance and discernment of tears in the Christian life. In the Western Catholic tradition, St Benedict put similar emphasis on it.

Long before the insights of modern psychology these wise pastor teachers understood the unique therapeutic power of tears in relating the unconscious and conscious parts of personality. Tears also heal and strengthen the psychosomatic unity of a person. They are a physical, bodily expression of a person's innermost spirit. But above all, tears are a profoundly important way in which the Holy Spirit works in the believer. For this reason tears have been spoken of as a continuation of our baptism, or a baptism of the Spirit. There are some similarities with the gift of tongues in this respect.[1]

Neglected gift

Tears are very commonly experienced where there is new awareness of God's Spirit. And the impact of the Pentecostal and charismatic movements in the Church – alongside the greater informality of our culture in general – has undoubtedly liberated many people into a new emotional freedom in their Christian life and worship (and goodness knows we needed it). But even at such times weeping is too easily understood as a response to a spiritual 'crisis', or simply part of healing ministry. It may be both those of course. But there is little awareness of the historic tradition in which this phenomenon stands in the Church. Few popular books on Christian prayer and theology give any attention to tears.[2] All of which means that the stress of the earlier Church teachers on this unpredictable emotion can sound very strange to Western ears: '. . . give me the tears of penance, loving tears out of love, tears of salvation, tears that clean the darkness of my mind, making me light so that I may see You, Light of world, Enlightenment to my repentant eyes'.[3]

Isaac the Syrian believed that tears were one of the first signs of God's grace at work in a person.

> When grace has begun to open your eyes so that they perceive things by means of precise vision, at that time your eyes will begin to shed tears until they wash your cheeks by their very abundance. If any one teaches you otherwise, do not believe him. To ask of your body

30

anything else apart from tears as an outward sign of reality, is not permitted to you.[4]

These were not the tears of a spiritual crisis or an emotional conversion experience. Isaac knew how to distinguish passing emotional moods from the presence of the Holy Spirit. He taught that tears were the truest measure of continued progress in the Christian life. To young monks he wrote:

> I am going to tell you something at which you must not laugh; for I am telling you the truth. Though you should suspend yourself by your eyelids before God, do not imagine that you have attained anything in your rule of life until you encounter tears; for until then your hidden self is still in the service of the world.[5]

The taming of tears

Pastoral and personal experience suggests that tears are *very* present in the lives of many people. But our social and spiritual inhibitions are deep and powerful and we often do not know how to recognize or honour them. Emotion has long been confused with emotionalism and we have forgotten how to tell the difference. Our culture has been taming or controlling grief for a long time. So it takes a lot of courage to allow our tears to flow, to risk expressing this emotion and perhaps discover God's Spirit within it. There may be many Christians who struggle to pray as they were taught, feeling unfulfilled and guilty because God is not more real to them, without any awareness or encouragement that their embarrassing capacity for weeping at every opportunity is in fact the gift of the Spirit to them.

Shortly after the funeral of her father, a woman came to a church service for the first time. She wept quietly throughout the service. She came the next week and the same happened again. It was some time before she was able to worship in church without tears. As the weeks went by it was clear that a new, deep and unexpected faith was being born in her. 'I know what was happening then,' she said, recalling the early weeks of tear-filled services. 'It was Jesus coming into my life.' Tears have continued to accompany her praying and worshipping. 'I don't feel sad,' she says. 'They come from deep inside me and I can't stop them.'

The language of tears

'Why are you weeping?' asked the angels. The question was not insensitive or mocking. Nor was Mary being criticized for a failure to rejoice in the resurrection. Tears are a language. We must learn to question them and listen to them. They need time and reverence. If we allow them to, they lead us to the true sources of our grief and burden. Once we have come to that place and have recognized and named our pain, we can begin to move on. Anyone involved in the pastoral care of the bereaved or traumatized knows the importance of the angels' question.

I remember once seeking out a pastoral friend to try and talk through a recurrent anxiety in my life. Barely into my story I found myself weeping helplessly. I ground to a halt, fumbling for my handkerchief and mumbling ritual apologies for crying. My friend sat quietly with me, neither embarrassed nor concerned to calm me down. My tears were not an intrusion. They were the reason I had come. When the storm of emotion had stilled, my friend spoke quietly and gently. 'Tell me about your tears.' I realized in that moment that my tears had revealed more of my fears than my words would ever have allowed. Far from getting in the way, my tears were my guide to meeting my pain.

This needs discernment. Our emotions are powerful and unpredictable and we learn to control and manipulate them. There may also be considerable confusion about guilt and responsibility in the cause of our grief. Tears can be merely sentimental. We can use them to manipulate sympathy and to influence situations for our own ends.

But when Jesus blesses those who mourn, he is blessing those who are willing to be truthful. They are people who mourn and lament life and death as they really are in this world. And the Christian community is commanded to share in such grieving. St Paul didn't say, '*Cheer up* those who weep.' He said, '*Weep* with them' (Romans 12.15). This is a very important insight. There can be no true rejoicing while at some level we are using it to avoid facing pain and grief.

One of the noticeable features of our society in times of tragedy is that people still expect the churches to know what to do with grief and to provide places where people can come.

Under pressure to be attractive and accessible to a culture increasingly uninterested in church it is perilously easy for Christian public worship to be endlessly upbeat and posi-tive and 'joyful'. Without a place for true grief and tears in Christian community, our search for joy and risen life will be dangerously superficial. The danger is that we may be simply copying the restless pursuit of our culture that runs to distraction and entertainment to avoid the sheer pain, exhaustion and confusion of much daily living.

It may be that people are looking for a place in which to grieve (whether or not they would actually express it this way), where their real tears and the heart of their longings will be heard with reverence and love.

It is only through death that we find resurrection. It is only through tears that we enter true joy.

Do not cling to me

It is probable that only those who have been through great tragedy can understand the desolation of Mary by the tomb. There comes a point in any bereavement when we can restrain ourselves no longer and our tears flow. For Mary, the final breaking point was that even the body had van-ished. Bitter despair, loss, hopelessness and utter confusion engulfed her in a flood-tide of grief.

But the story does not end in death.

Someone is standing behind her. He questions her. 'Woman, why are you weeping?' There is a beautiful meditation that draws out the real drama of this encounter.

Woman, why are you weeping? Whom are you looking for? The one you seek is in your possession, and you do not know it? You have the true, the eternal joy, and yet you weep? You stand outside, weeping at the tomb. Your heart is my tomb. And I am not dead there, but I take my rest in your heart, living for ever. Your soul is my garden. You were right to suppose that I was the gardener. I am the New Adam. I till and mind my paradise. Your tears, your love and your longing are all my work. In your inmost being you possess me, although you do not know it, and so you look for me without. Outwardly, therefore, I will appear to you, and so make you return to yourself, that in your inmost being you may find the one whom you seek outside.[6]

Now Jesus, the Second Adam, names his new creation: 'Mary'. She recognizes Jesus for the first time and flings herself on him. But he will not let her. 'Do not hold on to me, for I have not yet returned to the Father.'

It seems very harsh that in that moment of reunion Mary is so firmly pushed away. But she must let him go. There is a tough wisdom at work here. No relationship can survive when it is based on a fear of loss and death.

There is a tendency to place a lot of emphasis on the first

part of what Jesus said to Mary – 'Do not hold on to me.' The word also means 'cling'.

There is a tension here. The continual challenge of Christian faith is to deeper, closer involvement, expressed by varying degrees of practical involvement in the life of the Church. And where numbers and resources are scarce, the need is pressing. But any church leader knows the power of the opposite temptation. Trying to help individuals to see that their devotion to church activities (or career, work or relationships etc.) has become possessive and clinging can be one of the most painful tasks of pastoral ministry. However worthy and faithfully offered, 'religious' life can be peculiarly and fatally addictive for some.

It is not just Mary who needs to hear this command of Jesus.

Tears have something to do with a need to let go, or surrender. 'Tears are always a sign that we are struggling with power of one sort or another: the loss of ours; the entering of God's [. . .] The way and gift of tears opens the gate of death in this life to resurrection in this life. Tears release us from the prison of power and control into the vast love and infinite possibility of God.'[7]

But the actual reason Jesus gives for his insistence on not clinging is often forgotten. 'Do not hold on to me, *because I have not yet ascended to the Father*' (John 20.17, my italics). His mission is not yet complete. He has yet to ascend and take his throne. The Holy Spirit must be poured upon the Church. However tempting it may be for either of them, this was not the place to stop and rest.

He still has work to do – and so does Mary.

'Do not hold on to me. Go instead to my brothers and tell them, "I am returning to my Father and your Father, to my God and your God"' (John 20.17).

The end of tears

At the end of *The Lord of the Rings*, the last terrible battle won against all the odds, Sam the Hobbit is overcome with joy at the celebrations. He had dreamed of this moment through the darkest struggles of the days before.

> He laughed aloud for sheer delight, and he stood up and cried: 'O great glory and splendour! And all my wishes have come true!' And then he wept. And all the host laughed and wept, and in the midst of their merriment and tears the clear voice of the minstrel rose like silver and gold, and all were hushed. And he sang to them, now in the Elven-tongue, now in the speech of the West, until their hearts, wounded with sweet words, overflowed, and their joy was like swords, and they passed in thought out to regions where pain and delight flow together, and tears are the very wine of blessedness.[8]

Resurrection life will always be inseparable from tears. For to receive the new life of Christ must also awaken, in us as in him, our grief for what still lies dead in this world. The resurrection community is a community of blessed

37

mourners, longing for liberation but whose grief will not be comforted until all creation is restored in the gift of the risen Christ.

4

Stranger on the road

The walk to Emmaus

Now on that same day two of them were going to a village called Emmaus, about seven miles from Jerusalem, and talking with each other about all these things that had happened. While they were talking and discussing, Jesus himself came near and went with them, but their eyes were kept from recognizing him. And he said to them, 'What are you discussing with each other while you walk along?' They stood still, looking sad. Then one of them, whose name was Cleopas, answered him, 'Are you the only stranger in Jerusalem who does not know the things that have taken place there in these days?' He asked them, 'What things?' They replied, 'The things about Jesus of Nazareth, who was a prophet mighty in deed and word before God and all the people, and how our chief priests and leaders handed him over to be condemned to death and crucified him. But we had hoped that he was the one to redeem Israel. Yes, and besides all this, it is now the third day since these things took place. Moreover, some women of our group astounded us. They were at the tomb early this morning, and when they did not find his body there, they came back and told us that they had indeed seen a vision of angels who said that he was alive. Some of those who were

39

with us went to the tomb and found it just as the women had
said; but they did not see him.'

(Luke 24.13–24)

A pilgrim to the Holy Land today has a choice of four possible sites for the village of Emmaus. All are roughly the
right distance from Jerusalem, but beyond that nothing is
certain. Nor does it matter.

The significance of this story is not the place they were
going to, but what happened on the way.

On a road going west from Jerusalem, a couple are
walking slowly and despondently among the pilgrims
leaving the city after the Passover festival. A stranger over-
hears their conversation and asks them what they are
talking about.

They stop on the road, and begin to tell the stranger all
that is burdening them. Luke stresses their visible depression. Their story offers an insight into the reaction of the
disciples to the news of the resurrection. Far from being
good news, the report of the empty tomb, the experience of
the women and the vision of angels had simply added to the
pain, turmoil and tragedy of that whole weekend.

Perhaps it was all too much for this couple. Before Mary
arrived with the astonishing story of her actual meeting
with the risen Jesus, they had decided to go home.

It is a surprising situation. We have a tendency to believe
that the first disciples had an advantage over us because
they were *actually there as it happened.* But this couple
had followed Jesus, heard his teaching, seen his miracles,

40

witnessed his death and been told of his resurrection – and all without actually finding faith and spiritual understanding. For them, it had ended in death, not life. Seeing is not necessarily believing.

The irony is that in the moment they decide to walk away from Jesus, Jesus appears to walk towards them. This may be the clue to understanding the significance of the story.

Free gift

The Emmaus road makes explicit what all the other resurrection encounters hint at. To recognize Jesus and receive his new life is his gift alone. It is an awareness and understanding that cannot be arrived at by human will and reason alone. The helplessness and confusion of the disciples merely underlines that further.

The resurrection encounters are all the free acts of Jesus. This is in complete contrast to the events leading up to Easter. There he had allowed himself to be 'handed over'. He became a powerless human being and 'gave himself up' into the hands of those who betrayed and crucified him. Now in his risen life Jesus is in control of every encounter. He comes and goes at his own will. His presence cannot be demanded. He is only recognized when he chooses to reveal himself. He is beholden to no one. The fate of those demoralized disciples depends entirely on the predisposition of Jesus towards them. This is made quite explicit in his words at the end of Matthew's Gospel. On the mountain, Jesus claims the significance of his death and resurrection for the whole cosmic order: 'All authority in heaven and on earth has been given to me' (Matthew 28.18).

There is a sense of mischief running through this story that is easily missed because we don't expect the Bible to be mischievous! First, the two travellers are 'kept from' recognizing him. Jesus joins them on the road and plays the part of a friendly but ignorant stranger. He has apparently been staying in that small city, totally unaware that it was being rocked by religious and political crisis, culminating in the execution of a hugely popular spiritual leader. Even Cleopas is jolted out of his depression to ask him where he had been all weekend!

In drawing the story out of them, Jesus has the unusual experience of listening to his own obituary.

But the real encouragement of the story is that Jesus is there at all. He is deliberately seeking out two disciples who are walking away from it all.

There is a literary theory that all story-telling uses one of four plot-types, which correspond to the annual seasons. Tragedy corresponds to autumn, satire to winter, summer to romance. Applied to St John's Gospel the resurrection stories are the season of spring. Spring is the season of comedy. 'Comedy is inseparable from resurrection.'[1] Luke has caught the same mood.

Holy play

This divine playfulness simply underlines human power-lessness and incomprehension in the presence of God's activity. It is not for us to grasp – it is for God to reveal. There is no easy way to accept where this leads us. It means there is an innate insecurity to the experience of following Jesus. He is beyond our command and control. We can do nothing about it. This is very hard to accept. Christian faith, after all, encourages us to believe that God is with us and committed to us. He forgives us and hears and answers our prayers. He loves to reveal his ways to us. All of which is gloriously true. But it leaves us perilously tempted to treat God as if he has placed himself at our command and only finds his purpose in his involvement in our lives.

'We are so preoccupied with God's relatedness, God being for us, that we do not attend enough to God's hiddenness', writes Walter Brueggemann.[2]

There is a necessary 'hiddenness' in God's dealings with us. It is partly for our own protection. We would find it far too easy to take what is revealed and make it our final security. We would get in the way. This is not a jealous or resentful hiddenness. It is a loving concealment. As Rowan Williams so beautifully pictures it, 'Our lives are hidden in him, our deepest integrity and joy kept from our greedy eyes, drowned in his glory.'[3]

So any journey with Jesus will include a continuous encounter with our own blindness and with the idols we have made of our own 'understanding' and 'certainties'. In order for the disciples to recognize the risen Jesus they had first to suffer the loss of what they thought they knew about him. It may be that until that has happened Jesus is not just unrecognized, he is *unrecognizable*.

Jesus often taught that if we want to find life we must first be prepared to lose it. But we are probably never prepared for how final that losing must be. This story teaches us that there is a loss of faith and understanding that is necessary before we can recognize Christ in his new life.

There is no resurrection without a dying first.

In Chapter 2 I referred to an extended time I once spent in a mountain cabin. I had gone there to be alone. I thought there was nothing I wanted or needed more. But it was not what I expected. Once into the stillness of the mountains the experience became very unsettling. To my dismay the silence was empty. Even the most familiar comforts of faith and assurance went missing. It was a wilderness and I had no way of knowing how far it would stretch before me. I wept over God's absence. I protested and got very angry. This was a crisis of faith. How could I believe any more? Who was God anyway? And I began to realize the nature of my demands. The temptation to negotiate with God runs so deep.

God is gift. He cannot be commanded. Up there in that Alpine cabin one morning, there came a tearful and pro-found moment. Kneeling on the wooden floor I told God I would no longer treat him as if I owned him. Life was for him to give and for him to take away. I confessed my attempts to control and dominate. I 'let him go'. I asked for the life that was his gift alone. Of course we never learn such lessons once and for all. But something died that day – and something was born.[4]

I came to see that I had effectively tried to organize a

retreat for myself as if it were bookable, like a package holiday. My plans were doomed to disaster. I attempted to express the folly and confusion of attitude in a meditation called 'Swissair hermit'.

> Here I am God,
> scattered all over the Alps.
> No one reported the crash,
> rescuers will never find
> the pieces.
>
> I was on my way for a well-earned
> Package Solitude.
> Overloaded with thoughts and hopes
> I couldn't make the height.
> Lost all control, just
> broke up in mid-movie
> and fell to earth.
> No bomb suspected.
> None needed.
> Fatigue maybe.
>
> Search for the wreckage, God,
> find my black box.
> Somewhere in the deepest gorge,
> under pines and snow,
> battered, unconscious,
> lying where it fell,
> locked up with all

45

the mystery of who I was becoming
when it all began.

For more information on the crash, God
the emergency number to ring is:
020 (if you're outside London)
8811 7915
I'll repeat that,
020 (if you're outside London)
8811 7915.

Seen and unseen

Christian worship and prayer that celebrates only what is 'seen' and 'revealed' is always in danger of being shallow and superficial. The necessary corrective is found in the apophatic or 'Negative' theology taught in the Eastern Orthodox tradition. 'Hidden' is actually a better word for it. It is called 'Negative' in contrast to 'Positive' theology which affirms and asserts what is known and revealed about God. It reminds us that in the end God cannot be known by human understanding or reason. God is always beyond our capacity to imagine him, picture him, understand him or put him into human language. The only way is the way of *un*knowing.

The journey of faith towards God involves times when there is a loss of words, understanding and vision of God. They are not wrong in themselves. But they are limited and can easily mislead. The way of faith must include the gift of a darkness that exposes the emptiness of our concepts and ideas of God and of ourselves. It is a 'night of the senses' in which love and longing are all we have to offer. And that is all we need. 'Only loving can lead to the full knowledge that exceeds thought and words.'[5]

A recovery of this wisdom is vital for the health of the Church in Western society today. One contemporary writer on spiritual life stresses the need for a new reverence for the God who is hidden and dwells in mystery. Such a spirituality 'will seek to lead people away from a religion of easy answers into the dark night of faith. In an age of false certainties, of rigid fundamentalisms of various kinds, the renewal of mystical theology, the agnosia, the unknowing, is of the greatest importance'.[6]

The way of unknowing, the loss of understanding, is not intended to be a way of ignorance. Christian mysticism is not mindless.

> Then he said to them, 'Oh, how foolish you are, and how slow of heart to believe all that the prophets have declared! Was it not necessary that the Messiah should suffer these things and then enter into his glory?' Then beginning with Moses and all the prophets, he interpreted to them the things about himself in all the scriptures.
>
> (Luke 24.25–27)

On the Emmaus road Jesus hears their confession of confusion and roundly rebukes them for their unbelief and their lack of solid Bible study. 'Foolish' is a poor translation. He calls them 'dull' and 'slow', and the Greek here suggests that he speaks with strong emotion. Not for the first time, Jesus is exasperated by disciples who cannot grasp what to him is apparently obvious.

But it is not the resurrection he teaches them about. It is the cross and his sufferings.

Here Luke lets down his readers completely. He tells us that Jesus went through the entire Hebrew scriptures showing how they spoke of him, but for some reason omits to tell anyone what Jesus said! Christians ever since have been left with the frustrated feeling that this Bible study would have been the answer to so many questions.

But the challenge of Jesus' rebuke can be levelled just as easily at today's Church. The Old Testament has long suffered from neglect, careless reading or misuse at the hands of the Christian community.

The Church has struggled to read and listen to the Old Testament with the reverence, love and care that Jesus showed for it. Many struggle to find these scriptures believable today in the way that Jesus clearly expected of his disciples. Where the language and content are not simply too far removed from today's world and concerns, they may well sound harsh and intolerant. 'Dull' would sum up the opinion of many who have encountered these scriptures in public worship. And when they are not dull they sound irrelevant – or often offensive – to modern ears. Some published versions of the Psalms cope with the more vengeful and 'difficult' verses by putting the offending lines in brackets. Forewarned, we can choose not to disturb our devotions with those rough-edged searches for faith and meaning.

In such circumstances it is easier to dip into favourite passages, stories and psalms rather than strive to try and see the story as a whole. But while our knowledge of these scriptures revolves only around the safety and warmth of God's promises and blessings, the faith that results will be dull and slow of heart and Christ will remain a stranger.

So I wonder if the stress in Jesus' rebuke was on the word '*all* that the prophets have spoken'. To find the suffering and crucified God foreshadowed in 'all' the Old Testament requires a willingness to wrestle with the darker and more painful corners of what is written there. Even the disciples had not done that until they were forced to.

Living proof

'Beginning with Moses . . .' In some more conservative Christian traditions the Old Testament tends to be mined at this point as a resource for verses, teachings and 'proof texts' that appear to point to Christ. Did you know, for example, that the Old Testament contains over 300 references to the Messiah that were fulfilled by Jesus? Careful study is clearly encouraged by Jesus himself but we should beware of stating too certainly what the Bible chooses not to state directly. The Bible is not to be treated like a spiritual equivalent of a car maintenance manual. The Christian understanding of revelation is not finally of a written text, but of a living God.

On that road, Jesus told those two disciples that their

knowledge and trust in the Bible was inadequate. But we have no good reason for believing that he quoted 300 Old Testament proof texts at them. Nor did they need a study on the doctrine of the inspiration of the Bible. There are times when this approach to belief comes very close to a 'salvation by words'.

There are no direct, predictive statements in the Old Testament that anticipate a Messiah entering glory through suffering in the way that Jesus does. But it is through these same scriptures that Jesus led those two disciples to recognize the character of God in the midst of his world, finally and fully revealed in the sufferings of Christ.

The Bible is a meeting of both God's world and ours. We must recognize our own place in the stories that are written there. So what should be our response to those places where the Bible seems obscure, harsh or just impossible to understand? Rowan Williams writes:

> Must we not say something like the following? Scripture we know is not simply an oracle. It is not simply remarks dropped down from heaven and written on stone . . . we may be more helped by reflecting on the story of Jacob wrestling with the angel than by any images of oracles from heaven. Here in scripture is God's urgency to communicate, here in scripture is our mishearing, our misappropriating, our deafness and our resistance. Woven together in scripture are those two things, the giving of God and our inability to receive what God wants to give. On almost every

page of the gospels we read: 'Jesus said, "Do you understand?" They said, "No."'

We read with a sense of our own benighted savagery in receiving God's gift, and our solidarity with those writers of scripture caught up in the blazing fire of God's gift who yet struggle with it, misapprehend it, and misread it.[7]

As they came near the village to which they were going, [Jesus] walked ahead as if he were going on. But they urged him strongly, saying, 'Stay with us, because it is almost evening and the day is now nearly over.' So he went in to stay with them.

When he was at table with them, he took bread, blessed and broke it, and gave it to them. Then their eyes were opened, and they recognized him, and he vanished from their sight. They said to each other, 'Were not our hearts burning within us while he was talking to us on the road, while he was opening the scriptures to us?'

That same hour they got up and returned to Jerusalem.

(Luke 24.28–33)

When they reach Emmaus, Jesus behaves as if he is going to continue his journey. This may be more mischief on his part for he has yet to complete his ministry to this couple. But we may also recognize the courtesy of Christ. He does not force himself upon them. He does not presume his

51

invitation into their home. For the first time he waits for them to take the initiative.

His presence has captivated them, however, and they 'urge' him to stay.

At the meal table the moment comes for his revealing to them. He has carefully prepared them for this moment. He has walked with them, unseen. He has taught them from the scriptures and ministered to them by the gift of his Spirit burning within them as they walked. In a moment of moving intensity at the evening meal, he takes bread, blesses it and breaks it for them.

It is very significant that this should be the moment for their eyes to open. The risen Jesus can only be recognized as the same Jesus of the Last Supper. He is the suffering and crucified one who has now entered into glory.

Open eyes

In the moment of recognition he vanishes, but there is no despondency at this. At the beginning of the story his loss had left them desolate. Now it leaves them fulfilled. His ministry to them is complete. The rumour is confirmed. What was lost has now been found. His final gift to them is their recognition of themselves in all that has happened. 'Did not our hearts burn within us?' Their real journey can now begin.

For Gregory of Nyssa, a teacher firmly in the 'Hidden' tradition of theology, this losing and finding are one and the same thing in our encounter with God. It cannot be otherwise: 'To find God is to seek him unceasingly. Here to seek is not one thing and to find another. The reward of the search is to go on searching. The soul's desire is fulfilled by the very fact of remaining unsatisfied, for really to see God is never to have had one's fill of desiring him.'[8]

The Emmaus road story sustains the paradox of losing and finding, blindness and sight, to its very close.

5

Some of our women amazed us

Women, men and the subversiveness of resurrection

⟹▸◦◂⟸

Now after he rose early on the first day of the week, he appeared first to Mary Magdalene, from whom he had cast out seven demons. She went out and told those who had been with him, while they were mourning and weeping. But when they heard that he was alive and had been seen by her, they would not believe it.

(Mark 16.9)

The resurrection of Jesus from the dead was not the only event the disciples had to come to terms with on that first Easter Day. The first person Jesus chose to tell was a woman.

The news of the empty tomb broke upon the world as a rumour spread by women.

Anyone wanting to claim that these stories were made up by later Christians has got to explain the scandal of this central detail. In the culture of those days, no one inventing a resurrection story would start like this. And no one would be expected to believe it.

But if the word of Mary is true, God has done the unthinkable. God has cut right across all social and religious traditions of that time. In a world in which all authority was vested in men, God's greatest revelation is given to a woman. In a society where the testimony of a woman was not even accepted in a court of law, Jesus made a woman his apostle ('sent one') to the men. Mary deserves a unique honour. For a short while she was the only Christian witness in the world. God is being very subversive.

It is entirely predictable that such a witness should be dismissed out of hand by the men (at least initially): 'the story appeared to them to be nonsense' (Luke 24.11, REB). If God wanted to say something important, they thought it should be said to men.

Later that day, however, Cleopas admits to the stranger on the Emmaus road that the story had amazed them enough to check it. 'Some of those who were with us went to the tomb and found it just as the women had said' (Luke 24.22–24). But when the disciples meet in Jerusalem to confirm the discovery that Jesus has risen, it is not the women's witness that is celebrated. Their word is still without honour. 'It is true; the Lord has risen; he has appeared to *Simon*' (Luke 24.34, REB, my italics).

The same thing happens when St Paul writes to the Corinthian church about the death and resurrection of Christ. He lists all the appearances of Jesus to the male disciples, includes himself ('last of all'), but completely omits Mary and any of the women (1 Corinthians 15.3–8).

Silent witnesses

It is very clear from the Gospel accounts that Jesus was revolutionary in his friendship, openness and acceptance of women. It is less often noted how alive and liberated women were in relating to him. In John's Gospel alone women have a central part in nearly half the most significant scenes. Martha and Mary, Mary Magdalene, the woman at the well, all related to Jesus with a directness and vitality that was not evident among many of the men.

The women were also faithful to Jesus, staying with him through his suffering and crucifixion while all but John among the men had deserted.

But the Gospels themselves are almost totally the testimony and theology of men. In fact they hardly record the words of women at all.

So if we ask, 'How did the female disciples experience following Jesus and understand his teaching?' the answer is, 'We do not know.' They are never allowed to tell the story in their own words.

So there is always a gap, a silence, in the witness of the first Christian community. The story has only been heard from one side. We are left wondering.

Another example of the silence is the story of the appearance of Jesus to two disciples on the road to Emmaus, mentioned above and discussed more fully in the previous chapter. There has long been a curiosity about who the disciples were. Luke names one of them, Cleopas, in a way that suggests they would *both* have been known to his readers.

Cleopas also appears in John's Gospel as the husband of Mary, one of the women who stood by the cross.

But who was the other disciple? Throughout the story the other disciple is 'spoken for' in a way that culturally suggests a woman. Cleopas would not have been travelling with a woman other than his wife. Furthermore a woman would not be expected to speak to another man in public. Had the other disciple been a man he would surely have been named, whereas in the Gospels women are generally only named in their own right when no men are present. Finally, when they arrive at Emmaus the stranger is invited into their home ('stay with *us*', 29).

On these grounds it has long been thought likely that the other disciple was in fact Mary, his wife. They were an important family in the early Church. Their son Simeon became one of the first bishops of Jerusalem. The telling of this story would have had added significance to first generations of the new Church.

It means also that this silent listener on the road was one of the women at the cross. It is highly likely that she knew a great deal about the events at the tomb that morning. Perhaps she was there. Certainly the women would have talked together.

Of course we don't actually know. We are making connections. Trying to honour the witness of women in the New Testament has always had to involve some detective work and reconstruction, and I am not pretending otherwise. But there is a certain irony in picturing a depressed Cleopas relating second-hand stories about Jesus, to Jesus, in front of his wife who just might have known it all first hand anyway!

A different story

Whatever the faltering intentions of the first Christian community, for the greater part of the long history of the Church this one-sided witness became institutionalized. With a few exceptions, leadership, theology and worship have been solidly and jealously the work of men in the Church. Only slowly are we beginning to hear another side to the same story.

The painful irony of a Church that has left women feeling marginalized is that it has never solved the problem of absent men. An experienced spiritual director offers a telling insight into this situation from her experience of leading prayer and meditation groups. She encourages the members to imagine themselves at the cross. They are asked to picture the scene, the sounds, the light, the smells, the atmosphere. Then they watch the dying Christ, his wounds, his struggles to breathe . . . 'Now,' she says, 'you are there, what do you do?'

And the extraordinary thing is, that, almost without exception, men can't take it. They go away. They simply can't stand to watch that intensity of suffering. So they slope off. Women can't stand it either. But they are determined to save him. So they fling themselves at the cross to cut him free. Or they start rallying the crowds to take on the Roman soldiers. The one thing they can't manage in the face of such evident wretchedness, is inactivity.[1]

This tendency to walk away from emotionally difficult situations is a painful mark of the male in our culture. He disembodies himself from physical reality. He cuts out and finds himself unable to relate. The search for absent fathers demonstrates but one feature of that. A primary task for men in our society is to recover an awareness and accept-ance of their own bodily existence. One writer on mas-culine identity and spirituality suggests that the male recovery of the body will lead to a 'recovery of resurrection faith'. Resurrection faith is always a resurrection of the *body*.

The word of a woman

The New Testament writings themselves reflect the tension and confusion of a Church trying to live faithfully with a new vision for the partnership of women and men. The word and example Jesus left was disturbingly radical and far-reaching.

Old ways of thinking keep re-surfacing. Soon after greet-ing men and women as co-leaders in his churches, and despite declaring that in Christ there is 'neither Jew nor Greek, male nor female', St Paul goes on calling his readers 'brothers' and encouraging them as '*sons* of God'. That his writing and sermon-illustrations appear to be almost exclusively drawn from the world of men – wrestling, boxing, athletics for example – further highlights the problem.

Old habits die hard, even in the resurrection life.

We don't know, for example, if anyone suggested that Mary Magdalene might be on the short list to replace Judas among the apostles. She had everything on the job description but the right gender. Perhaps it was argued 'the time was not right'. At the end of the letter to the Romans, however, in a long list of warm greetings to women and men in the church there, we find St Paul personally greeting 'Andronicus and *Junias*' (a woman), telling us they have been in prison with him for the faith and that 'they are outstanding among the *apostles*'. He names a woman among the apostles.[2]

It is clear that women ministered, prophesied, taught and took authority alongside men in the resurrection Church.

In first-century Hebrew and Greek cultures such a partnership must have needed courage and a wise flexibility. There was always the risk of confusion and misunderstanding.

While it is also true that there are teachings that apparently contradict each other over the place and ministry of women in the Church, a belated awareness has been growing that the Church has been applying these teachings without a full understanding of the original context in which they were written.[3]

Breaking silence

This is not an abstract theological debate. The social conse-
quences of this division have been devastating down the
centuries, and continue to cause suffering across the world
today.

Even now in the United Kingdom, after years of cam-
paigning, the average wages for women in the UK remain
significantly lower than for men, while the demands of
home and childcare remain almost as great as ever. In the
event of the breakdown of marriage, it is women who
make up the majority of one-parent families. Research
shows that a fairly constant 60 per cent of such families are
living at below half the average income. In times of economic recession it is women who bear the brunt of the
sacrifices. Women wanting to pursue a career are still
expected to juggle work and family responsibilities at the
same time.

Globally the picture is even more alarming. The Nobel
Prize-winning economist Amartya Sen has researched
world population figures and published her findings under
the title 'More Than 100 Million Women are Missing'.[4]
Although the gender balance is generally maintained in
Western societies, she found that across the world the
picture is radically different. The traditional preference for
the male, patriarchal assumptions about role and lifestyle
and economic burden of social practice means that women
(if they survive birth) are likely to be less wanted and loved,
be fed and treated less well from birth, will lack education

and will be given less access to basic health care. Where resources are scarce, it is the male who takes priority.

As one person observed, 'To be born of a woman is plain fact. To be born a woman has been for the most part a misfortune.'[5]

The witness of the Christian partnership of men and women in the new life of the kingdom suddenly takes on a new perspective.

New man, new woman

The Church that began with the calling of a woman on resurrection day has still far to go to honour and witness to the partnership it is called to. The stories of women in the faith can still be relatively neglected or excluded from the Christian community. In the Christian Calendar used by the Church of England the number of men honoured as saints or godly examples still wildly outnumbers women (a claim to raise the eyebrows of more impartial observers of human behaviour). The more extensive Roman Catholic list reveals the same proportionate bias. It is clear that in the process of recognizing sanctity, sexual politics is at least as influential as holy living.

Only recently has the cycle of Sunday and daily scripture readings chosen for public worship been revised. In this cycle many of the most glorious and positive stories of women's faith, obedience and initiative have until now been missing. This means that regular worshippers at traditional Anglican services had not been hearing the word and witness of faithful women alongside those of men from the Bible. By contrast, most of the stories of 'fallen' and 'sinful' women were included.

Take the moving story of the woman anointing Jesus with expensive perfume. All four Gospels record it, but only Luke mentions that she is a known sinner in that community and stresses her need for forgiveness (Luke 7.36ff). Mark and Matthew record the other side of that story – that her anointing of Jesus was a powerful prophetic ministry to Jesus and he gloriously affirms her – 'She has done a beautiful thing . . . wherever the gospel is preached in the whole world, what she has done will be told in memory of her' (Mark 14.6b, 9, RSV).

Well, except in the Church of England that is. Luke's story of the forgiven prostitute has long been a Sunday eucharistic reading. Mark's account, to be told 'wherever the gospel is preached' was only set for reading on a Tuesday morning in January.

Of course the situation is not helped by the fact that the disciplined use of the lectionary is itself in decline in many local churches. A church that only reads aloud stories of *fallen and sinful* women is not likely to find the suggestion of women in leadership very compelling.

The lack of women's experience impoverishes much of our liturgy as well. This is never more evident than in the liturgy of baptism. When Jesus wants to describe how God brings us to new life he speaks of the wonder and vulnerability of a baby being born out of its mother's womb. We are born out of the womb of God's love (John 3.3). But in the

Anglican baptism service the water is blessed with the more impersonal symbols of washing dirt away, of the Red Sea parting and of the dark waters of death. But the picture most precious to the experience of Jesus, and most fundamental to our experience – childbirth – is only mentioned in curiously detached, factual terms.[6]

Healing the split

When Jesus asks to receive the news of the resurrection from the lips of a woman he is asking us to listen very carefully. In a society where women were always followers, he chose a woman to lead. In a culture that required women to be silent, Jesus gave them a message to proclaim. In a world where women were treated as second class, he rose to greet them first.

It is evident that the Christian Church for most of its history has been unable to recognize the implications of the example of Jesus in this resurrection sign. Although the message of Easter was heard through the voice of a woman, their voice and ministry has more often been refused in the mission of the gospel.

Whether men have been any more fulfilled in their persistent denial of genuine partnership with women in the ministry of the gospel is an open question. But there is surely a price to be paid for trying to carry the whole story of humanity alone. Theology and history have been written as if 'male' experience was universal experience. The fact is that it never has been. The recovery of the partnership of men and women does not only offer women the possibility of new recognition and fulfilment. Men too will encounter their own identity in a new light.

In the Church of England the first women were ordained priest in 1994. Women now make up approximately 20 to 25 per cent of all ordained ministers, and 50 per cent of those currently in training for ordained ministry. But the issues remain significantly unresolved and result in very painful tensions. As an institution, the Church's employment practice allows discrimination on the basis of gender. A local church can legally refuse the ministry of a woman (but not a man). It is a situation that would be considered scandalous if the discrimination was being made on the basis of colour rather than gender.

There is abundant evidence of the fruitfulness and enrichment that women bring to ministry in the Church given the opportunity. But listening to the stories of gifted women colleagues in ordained ministry I observe how many struggle to articulate quite why their experience of ministry within the Church feels so costly and painful. Of course it can be tough for men too, but this is something to do with the experience of being a woman in ministry in a Church long functioning as a male-led institution in which the validity and theological integrity of a woman's call is still, effectively, held in question.

One woman priest has written of her experience of living and working in a theological training college community:

A feeling somehow grew that, in the texts of theology, my women students and I did not exist. Something important about us and our lives had not gone into forming this rich doctrinal, liturgical and pastoral mixture. Somehow women's voices had not been heard, and we were all the losers for it.

I remember thinking on one particularly grim day, 'It doesn't matter, because God loves women!' – and somehow, and to my surprise, this recognition made me weep with relief. Of course, I had never consciously doubted that God loved women. But somehow the barrage of ancient opinion, the structures into which one was perceived to fit oddly, the little niggling [. . .] negativities which one felt in a place which fitted the male candidates like a glove, all conspired to make one feel that women were not really quite as good as men, that God didn't care about women *quite* as much as men, that women's sufferings (so many of them not even figuring on the ethics or pastoral courses) did not matter *quite* as much as those of men, that what happened to women in the home didn't matter *quite* as much as what happened to men in the work-place. In short, that somehow women didn't figure except as sources of gynaecological problems in Christian ethics, or people to make tea.[7]

I hope they said sorry

I hope they said sorry – those male disciples. I need to say sorry too, somehow, somewhere.

It needs saying. Sorry that we have been so slow to believe. Sorry for not naming those we journeyed with. Sorry that whole dimensions of human experience have been excluded from worship and prayer. That so much of the masculine inheritance in the faith has been the privileged fruit of deep, sustained injustice, a wilful rejection, unbelief and a need to control. Sorry for the refusal to believe the word of a woman on that Easter morning. I repent of my sins.

But we should not be surprised that this particular journey to risen life is so long and painful. The Bible is clear that the division between men and women is second only to the division between God and his world.

God is not overturning one hierarchy to replace it with another. He is calling women and men to a new relationship.

If this is the place where the Church of England has now come to, no one can accuse it of hurrying. It was highly appropriate that, rather than ordaining women priests on the traditional feast days of the very male and hierarchical St Peter or the great Archangel Michael, the Diocese of London held its services on the same weekend as the London Marathon!

'It is true: the Lord has risen; he has appeared to *Mary*.'

6

This is flesh
I'm talking about here!

The resurrection of the body

<hr>

While they were talking about this, Jesus himself stood among them and said to them, 'Peace be with you.' They were startled and terrified, and thought that they were seeing a ghost. He said to them, 'Why are you frightened, and why do doubts arise in your hearts? Look at my hands and my feet; see that it is I myself. Touch me and see; for a ghost does not have flesh and bones as you see that I have.'

While in their joy they were disbelieving and still wondering, he said to them, 'Have you anything here to eat?' They gave him a piece of broiled fish, and he took it and ate in their presence.

(Luke 24.36–39, 41–43)

In the novel *Towing Jehovah*,[1] God has died of unknown causes and his body has fallen from heaven into the Atlantic Ocean just south of the equator. The archangels want him to have a proper burial. The Vatican realizes the need for secrecy. A huge super-tanker is chartered to find the body and tow it to a remote tomb under the North Pole. As this subversive comedy unfolds, a motley crew of sailors, theologians, atheists and feminists alike struggle with this challenge to some of their core beliefs and unbeliefs about God. That God *existed* after all. That God was *male*. That he has *died*. That God had a *body*.

The whole dark comedy unfolds as the divine corpse, over two miles long, is slowly being towed towards the Arctic by its ears.

Out of the body

One of the earliest theological arguments in the first Christian Church was whether Jesus came as a real, physical human being. A very early test of true faith was whether the believer was willing to confess that Christ came in the flesh (1 John 4.2), rather than just wearing humanity like a cloak to cover his real, all-powerful divinity.

The same issue surfaces when faced with the apparently solid flesh of the risen Jesus. At fairly regular intervals through church history the arguments are set off again, provoked, perhaps, by a film, a new book or an interview with the maverick theologian of the day.

On one level it is hardly surprising if the body of Jesus provokes questions. The Christian faith has never been sure what to make of *anyone's* body particularly. A perverse and destructive dualism between 'spirit' and 'matter' has infected so much of the understanding of the Church that we have been left with little positive use for the body at all. It has often been treated as a burden to be towed around in this mortal life while the 'spirit' within longs for its freedom. 'The flesh' has always been an embarrassment or an enemy. The phrase itself instantly conjures up something forbidden and illicit. Life in the body is to be endured rather than celebrated.

The really important parts of the Christian life are 'spiritual' – such as worship and prayer. So, not surprisingly, 'it is difficult to be on equally good terms with God and your body'.[2]

Of course it is never spelled out so crudely but we learn this split in all sorts of ways. For example, as a child in Sunday school I learned that in order to pray and be with God, the body had to be kept still – 'Hands together, eyes closed'. In those days, before more informal approaches to worship became the pattern, our bodies were really an irrelevance to the 'real' purpose of being in church. So like resentful children, dragged by the ears and knowing instinctively where they are not really welcome, they made continuing protest. They fidgeted and ached on those hard unforgiving pews, groaned on the prayer kneelers apparently filled with concrete, coughed and shivered beside the labouring Victorian heating system and generally made themselves a thoroughly temporal nuisance.

Those without experience of being a church-going teenager will not have memory of certain embarrassing evenings at Christian youth camps – the 'relationship talk'. Here I was told that my body was full of awkward and powerful passions (a discovery I had already made). I learned that these were wonderful but wrong and needed strictly controlling in case I enjoyed them.

Having taken my turn at giving those talks, I am much more compassionate towards those brave leaders now: the struggle to offer a responsible alternative to the growing hedonism of the prevailing culture was a real issue. But it was hard not to come over as negative or reactive in all this. Though no one ever claimed that marriage was a remedy against lust (as the old Prayer Book said), there was a perceptible anxiety behind all this which would clearly only be relieved when we were all 'safely' married.

In confirmation classes I learned that my body was the 'Temple of the Holy Spirit' – which never honestly sounded very exciting and seemed to be all about behaviour and little to do with pleasure. 'Life in the Spirit', at that stage, had all the attraction of disinfectant.

It is not surprising that in such a church we pray with eyes shut. For 'spiritual life' requires becoming *less* aware of the things of earth. 'Holiness is tantamount to bodilessness and saints are sexless people, mystically attuned to a life transcending earthly matter.'[3] No, not sex*less*, so much as sex-*denying*. Until very recently the word 'virgin' was written alongside the names of holy women (but not men) in the church calendar of saints – as if no other detail of their lives was needed to explain their sanctity. Saint = no sex; holiness = spirit.

Is it really surprising that a church so unsettled by its own fleshly reality should be unsure how to respond to the risen, glorified flesh of God?

Written on the body

The Christian faith is incurably and unavoidably physical. It has been rightly described as the most materialistic of all religions. It is faith in a God who has taken flesh and made his home in our physical, earthly nature. So Christian faith can never be about the liberating of our 'spirit' out of 'flesh'. It is about the hope of the union and transformation of spirit *and* matter, made one and whole in the love of Christ. Such a faith should change the way we relate to our own bodies. It is holy stuff, this flesh and blood: God has taken it as his own.

The Gospel stories clearly emphasize the physical reality of the risen Jesus. Indeed, they go out of their way to stress this. In fact, popular Jewish belief at that time would not have assumed that resurrection was anything other than bodily. To be sure, it was a body with new 'agilities'.[4] Jesus could appear and disappear at will. He was also very diffi-cult to recognize until he chose to reveal himself. He could overhear conversations at which he was not physically present.

But in front of startled and frightened disciples Jesus went out of his way to assure them that it was really him ('. . . it is I myself' – Luke 24.39) and to demonstrate to them the solidity and reality of his physical nature ('give me something to eat'). The disciples at Emmaus never ques-tioned that they had travelled with a real human being. Mary in the garden, even out of traumatic grief, never doubted that she was talking to a real person. We note that she clung to him physically and had to be asked to let go. Finally Thomas was invited to physically touch Jesus' wounds.

But this is surely consistent with the story that has gone before. God has always been delighted in physical things. This God has always chosen to express himself through physical things. He created this universe. He came and lived, suffered and died in our flesh. And it is in this flesh that he has now risen from death to new life.

We have to remain reverently agnostic about what the texts do not attempt to tell us. The risen Jesus is not physically described at all. We don't know what he looked like. The curiosity is natural. He had left his grave-clothes, for example, so was he naked when he appeared to the disciples? The thought was a little too much for St Bernard who had to reassure anxious readers that in the event 'the eye of love clothes the vision in familiar garments'![5]

What is plain from all the accounts is that disciples were left in no doubt that they were meeting a physical human being. Someone who can pass through walls, appearing and disappearing, is normally assumed to be *less* substantial – ghost or apparition. C. S. Lewis suggested that the 'agility' of the risen Jesus reveals that the life he has entered in our flesh is actually *more* real and solid than ours – not less.[6]

The ancient Easter liturgies of the Church have always celebrated the resurrection with very physical and sensual imagery. They use the language of marriage and the wedding night. The Easter tomb is our tomb. Christ comes to the tomb as a bridegroom. He comes to the death of our earthly nature and brings it to life. The tomb becomes a bedroom. So the resurrection has been described as 'the consummation of the marriage of heaven and earth'.

That God has this quite improbable love affair with our physical nature is beyond our imagining. But he clearly does. As one writer puts it – 'God's desire is revealed in our bodies. After all, what the doctrine of the incarnation whispers to us is that God, eternally, wants a body like ours. Have you ever thought about this . . . our body, as something that God desires?'[7]

And what *do* we think about it? How would we feel standing naked in front of a mirror, or lying in the bath, reading those words aloud: 'God wants a body like ours.'

Body shopping

That the hope of resurrection should include our physical bodies may come as a liberating thought. After all, we live in a culture that forces upon us impossible expectations, and our bodies carry the burden of them. The powerful multinational advertising industry deliberately exploits our physical unease. It constantly parades before us models of impossible physical perfection. While lifestyle choices have never been greater, so too are levels of stress-related illness and eating disorders. Something in all this leaves us deeply dis-eased.

In our consumer culture the body is exploited ruthlessly. So it absorbs all the burdens of our emotional and spiritual dis-ease. And in our despair we make impossible demands upon it to present us to the world with the images we think we need. In terms of our treatment and attitude to the body in our culture there may be very little to choose between the pornographic poster and an advertisement for a washing-up liquid.

In such a world the belief that God is intimately involved in our flesh has radical implications. Rubem Alves suggests that the loss of this belief leaves us free to exploit the body. 'For if God is found beyond the body, anything can be done to the body.'[8]

So to find God physically at home in the very part of our nature that leaves us alienated and abused is itself a gift to a world like ours. But the New Testament has no interest in image and looks in the way that obsesses our culture. We are never told what Jesus looked like. But it is the ground of our hope that this is a God who, without embarrassment, is willing to share our image and likeness and make his home among us.

Body positive

In fact our culture has been showing a new attentiveness and sensitivity towards the body in recent years. There is an awareness that it is part of the whole person and should be treated with love and respect.

Health and fitness centres have appeared everywhere. Alternative health remedies have stressed the healing power of physical touch (such as in massage), and the use of the senses to reduce stress (such as aromatherapy). Lifestyle and diet have become more important. Body-positive therapies have claimed much success in treating serious illness through helping people discover a more healthy relationship with their physical bodies. This has been especially important where viruses such as AIDS have left sufferers facing actual rejection in their bodies.

A feature of the extraordinary variety of alternative spiritualities and meditation systems that are now a feature of our society is how much they creatively involve the body. This can become another form of exploitation or idolatry and a highly lucrative 'health and awareness' industry feeds this fascination for those who can afford it.

It needs approaching with care and discernment. But there is surely a deeper hunger behind all this. It is a longing to live whole in a world that divides us up so crudely.

Beginning as some-body

Where the body and spirit are recognized together in relating to God, there is new life. There is resurrection. It brings a quite new vitality. That is why I believe in the resurrection of the body.

For many this has to begin with a willingness to recognize our own bodies and 'own' them for the first time. Many people feel very ill at ease with their bodies and effectively ignore them. When leading prayer groups or retreats I sometimes suggest that individuals go to their room and explore the experience of praying to God naked. The idea is always greeted with nervous laughter. And people are always surprised by how much courage it actually takes to do it.

One person wrote to me of their experience.

> I locked the door and drew the curtains and lay naked on my bed. It felt very, very strange. I contemplated each part of my body. I tried to be aware of how I felt about it. All sorts of feelings surfaced as I did so. There were tears and there was laughter.
>
> Bit by bit I offered myself, bodily, to God – *for the first time* [my italics]. It still felt very strange. Over the next few weeks I kept praying that way until the strangeness passed. It was a profound and very important thing to have done.

Another participant spoke movingly of how the experience had not only released him into a new awareness of God's love, it had also brought him new-found sexual freedom in his marriage. We should not be surprised. In the affirming of our bodies as good, our deepest needs are ministered to and released. Christian spirituality is marked by a journey *toward* the flesh. It requires that we become more physical, not less. We are followers of Jesus – in his incarnation and resurrection.

There is another place where this truth is acted out very dramatically. Whenever times of spiritual renewal or revival come to the Church in its history, it is marked by an awakening of the body. The Spirit gives life to the flesh. The charismatic and Pentecostal movements of the last 30 years

offer many examples of this. It can take many forms, sometimes very dramatic and even eccentric. There can be falling
down, trembling, strong expression of laughter or tears. But
more often it has been marked by a gentleness and a very
moving awareness of God's presence filling body and soul.

In one such meeting I remember thinking that this all
looked, with widely varying degrees of excitement, like a
long overdue reunion of body and spirit.

With our whole being

Christian teaching on prayer and meditation is now
encouraging a much more positive place for the body. We
do not come to God as no-bodies. The word is very revealing. To be a no-body in our society is to be unrecognized –
not a real person. We relate as bodies. And what Jesus
affirms is that when we come to God we don't come to God
as *no*-bodies, or *any*-bodies. We come as *some*-bodies. He
calls us by name.

There has also been a greater confidence to allow our
senses to be part of our awareness of life and God. We are
allowed to pray with eyes open, taking in the created world.
We can taste, feel, watch and smell and listen. We are more
open to exploring what it might mean to live being fully,
passionately open to God rather than praying from within a
narrow idea notion of our 'spirit'.

If our praying has been inhibited by the need for special
language and phrases, the discovery that we can pray
through our bodies – expressing our prayers through

simple actions and not words – may be wonderfully liberating. And if our bodies carry the burdens and wounds of being neglected, ignored or even abused, the discovery that they can lead us into prayer and are reverenced in Christ can be deeply healing.

Love it, love it hard

The novelist Toni Morrison has often written of the importance of the body to peoples struggling to discover their own life and destiny out of oppression. 'Love your body' is a strong theological theme in her writing in a way that always combines protest and celebration (as perhaps the resurrection does too). In *Beloved*, Baby Suggs preaches to her slave congregation:

In the silence that followed, Baby Suggs, holy, offered up to them her great big heart.

She did not tell them to clean up their lives or to go and sin no more. She did not tell them they were the blessed of the earth, its inheriting meek or its glory-bound pure.

She told them that the only grace they could have was the grace they could imagine. That if they could not see it, they would not have it.

'Here,' she said, 'in this place, we flesh; flesh that weeps, laughs; flesh that dances on bare feet in grass. Love it. Love it hard. Yonder they do not love your flesh. They despise it. They don't love your eyes; they's just as soon pick 'em out. No more do they love the skin on your back. Yonder they flay it. And O my people, they do not love your hands. Those they only use, tie, bind, chop off and leave empty. Love your hands! Love them. Raise them up and kiss them. Touch others with them, pat them together, stroke them on your face 'cause they don't love that either. *You* got to love it, *you*! And no, they ain't in love with your mouth. Yonder out there, they will see it broken and break it again. What you say out of it they will not heed. What you scream from it they do not hear. What you put into it to nourish your body they will snatch away and give you leavins instead. No, they don't love your mouth. *You* got to love it. This is flesh I'm talking about here. Flesh that needs to be loved. Feet that need to rest and dance; backs that need support; shoulders that need arms, strong arms I'm telling you. And O my people, out yonder, hear me, they do not love your neck unnoosed and straight. So love your neck; put a hand on it, grace it, stroke it and hold it up.'[9]

Postscript

After I finished writing this chapter I began to store it on the computer. Each chapter is stored under one word from its title. My computer shows a rare flash of human intuition. On the screen it asks the question.

'Save flesh before closing?' Yes/No.

Of course. That's what this chapter is all about.

7

The wounds that keep us

The risen presence of Jesus

When it was evening on that day, the first day of the week, and the doors of the house where the disciples had met were locked for fear of the Jews, Jesus came and stood among them and said, 'Peace be with you.' After he said this, he showed them his hands and his side. Then the disciples rejoiced when they saw the Lord. Jesus said to them again, 'Peace be with you. As the Father has sent me, so I send you.' When he had said this, he breathed on them and said to them, 'Receive the Holy Spirit.'

(John 20.19–22)

Something strange is going on when a crowd of people start celebrating at the sight of a scarred and wounded body. When did the sight of someone disfigured or tortured last fill you with joy?

Something strange is going on when it is a glorified but *wounded* man who stands before us on the day of resurrection. Surely a victorious body like Christ's, a body that has conquered sin and death, that has broken out of the grave with radiant new life, will be whole and without blemish?

But not only is his body still scarred, it is those same wounds by which the disciples recognize Jesus and are overcome with joy.

Nor are these scars that are left over from a previous battle. They are not the cuts and bruises of a Hollywood hero who emerges victorious against impossible odds. They will not heal in time. These are the wounds of the cross. They are the terrible wounds of human betrayal, of torture, humiliation, degradation and of an agonizing death.

Were there other marks still on him? Was his nose still broken, his faced puffed and bruised from the beatings? Was his head still gashed from the thorns?

We don't know. But those five scars – from the spear and the nails – have come to symbolize all Christ's earthly sufferings.

And those are the marks found on the body of the risen, all-conquering, victorious Christ. The cross, it seems, has left Christ wounded for eternity.

Glorious scars

The risen Jesus was recognized by his scars. This story unites the resurrection with the cross. The one who has risen is the one who was crucified. Resurrection life never moves on from the cross as if it can be left behind. Rather, it reveals the cross as a victory.

Resurrection life is none other than the way of the cross. Jesus makes this quite clear.

But John's story now goes further. It is the wounded and

victorious Christ who gives the Holy Spirit to the Church. He breathes the Holy Spirit on the disciples and commissions them with the continuation of his own work. 'As the Father has sent me, so I send you.'

This is where John tells of the gift of the Spirit. His picture of Pentecost contains what I would call a 'saving contradiction'. Pentecost, for John, is found in the place where the crucified, wounded one is recognized as the risen Lord.

By contrast, Pentecostal and charismatic renewal movements have tended to draw their theology of the cross and Pentecost through Luke's more linear, chronological account. This has often resulted in an unhelpful separation of cross and Pentecost as if the Christian community leaves the former behind and 'moves on' into the latter (illustrated by the early use of two-stage language such as '*second* blessing' to speak of the renewing experience of the Holy Spirit). An understanding of renewal shaped by John's 'holistic' theology of cross, resurrection and Spirit will be less prey to insensitive triumphalism, more centred on the cross and less easily distracted by the 'consolations' and manifestations that accompany the presence of the Spirit.[1]

In practice the struggle to hold together the 'saving contradiction' of cross and resurrection, defeat and victory, is too much for us. We end up emphasizing one truth at the expense of the other.

This is clearly revealed in Christian hymn books. There are large sections on the suffering and passion of Christ and large sections on resurrection and ascension. But very few hymns ever attempt to bring the two together. It is disturbing to note that hardly any popular resurrection hymns celebrate the risen *and wounded* Christ. Rather, resurrection life is set in direct contrast to the life of earth and the suffering of the cross. 'The head that once was crowned with thorns, is crowned with glory now.'[2]

Almost alone of all the established hymn writers, Charles Wesley returns again and again to celebrate Christ risen and wounded. Central to his vision of the returning Christ at the end of time are the marks of the cross.

> Those dear tokens of his passion
> still his dazzling body bears,
> source of endless exultation,
> to his ransomed worshippers,
> with what rapture,
> gaze we on those glorious scars.[3]

He is the exception, and many modern hymn books omit this verse. In popular devotion wounds and resurrection are kept clearly separate. At different times in the history and life of the Church we find one truth emphasized at the expense of the other.

God's visitation

In a church where I used to worship, there was a stained-glass window of Christ on the cross. The window was narrow so the hanging figure looked strangely squeezed. He was thin and gaunt. His face was exhausted and lifeless. He actually looked like the victim of a long and debilitating illness rather than a crucifixion. The image was literally sickening.

But what made the window so striking was the fact that the local council had placed a neon street light on the road directly outside the window. At evening services during the winter, the dying, emaciated body of Christ glowed down on us, bathing the congregation with a sickly shade of luminous green.

Where Christ's wounds are expressed in isolation from his resurrection a particular view of human suffering emerges. The rediscovery of the healing, transforming work of Christ is still relatively recent. For the last 400 years the Church of England officially taught the faithful to expect the opposite. The Book of Common Prayer was quite explicit about this. In the liturgy for use when visiting the sick there are no prayers for healing – only for endurance and patience. The priest states quite categorically, 'Whatsoever your sickness is, know you certainly, that it is God's visitation.' The sickness was God's 'fatherly correction', to add 'seriousness to his/her repentance'. The pastoral advice that followed included making a will![4]

Where there is no expectation of the possibility that God might break in and heal, the only alternative is to invest that suffering with divine meaning. This view is still widely held among Christians (though never stated so starkly).

I was once asked to lead a discussion for a healing prayer

group. In my talk I spoke about the risen Christ showing the disciples his wounds. I suggested that this was a source of hope in our own wounds. I tried to encourage a vision of the risen Christ ministering through the very things that leave us defeated and leading us to new life and healing. I tried to speak of the possibility of the victory of Christ's love in and through our own wounds and struggles.

The discussion that followed was dominated by stories about people who were struggling courageously through terrible illness and tragedy. I had no reason to disbelieve them. The way people seem to manage through appalling adversity is fearfully moving and a mark of God's grace.

The group had asked me to speak about healing. But they spoke constantly about suffering. Devoted and caring though the members of that group were, I came to believe that they were deeply confused in their vision of the wounded and *victorious* Christ. In the end there was no hope of healing – only of redemptive suffering. The healing service that followed had the feel and expectancy of an intensive care ward.

The mystique of suffering

In such a context, the question Jesus once asked a blind beggar is very important. 'What do you want me to do for you?' (Mark 10.51). It may be that the risen, wounded Christ asks the same question.

In the cult film *The Life of Brian*, there is a scene in which Brian passes a row of filthy beggars and crippled people in a Jerusalem market. In the middle of them is an obviously healthy man in a brilliant white loincloth. He is calling out 'Penny for an ex-leper.' He then complains loudly how he was making quite a good living as a leper until someone called Jesus came along and healed him.

The truth is that we can grow to love our wounds. In a perverse way they become our source of security. They set limits to our lives and we know where we are with them. We can even safely complain about them! They become the means by which we relate and establish our place in the community. A community that is preoccupied by a perverse 'love' of its wounds is one that will have no desire to grow. Strangely at home with suffering, it will find any gift of healing and new life very disturbing. In a way that may be hard to admit too, suffering can give us a significance and power we crave.

A body like yours

If the cross can be emphasized without resurrection, resurrection can also be emphasized without the cross.

In a church located in the same city as the one I referred to earlier was a quite different picture of Christ. Here he was the risen and victorious Christ. He was pictured as if sitting on an invisible throne, filling the wide east window. One hand was raised in blessing, the other extended in a gesture of greeting or instruction. His crowned head had blond hair, and deep-blue eyes gazed down upon the church. His naked body was powerfully muscular, radiantly handsome and enviably fit. A red robe discreetly trailed across his loins. He had no wounds upon him. Standing demurely in the window of the Lady Chapel was a very beautiful unblemished, blue-eyed Virgin Mary with long blond hair. She was holding a beautiful, blond-haired, blue-eyed baby boy.

This appalling confusion of muscularity for Christianity presents Christian life as an impossible ideal. Before that window I felt the same sense of inadequacy and hopelessness that I once experienced on a misguided visit to the gymnasium of a local health club. The Christ in that stained-glass window was already a creature remote from and beyond my own feeble humanity. His victory was unsurprising because he knew no human weakness. He was quite unmarked by any experience of this frail and violent world. He had left all that behind him. To be faithful to such a vision of Christ, the Church must exclude anything that contradicts it.

Faith based on such a vision leaves us in precisely the dilemma that made Jesus so angry with the institutional religion of his day. He passionately felt the injustice of religion that made impossible and condemning demands on people while offering no support for those who tried to respond.

'Religion is very good at describing the vision from the mountain tops,' said Rabbi Lionel Blue. 'It is never very good at telling us how to live in the valleys below.'

The age-old divisions of the Church have not helped either. Expressing a common suspicion of Protestants towards 'Catholic' devotions to Christ, I once heard a preacher criticizing Christians who used crucifixes rather than empty crosses for their devotions. 'Christ is not still on the cross,' he argued. 'He has risen.' I remembered because I was struggling with depression at the time. Believing was very hard but I had found no way of sharing my struggles with anyone in that church. The whole place felt so positive and full of resurrection that I felt I would be letting the side down.

The only thing I knew was that my cross was not empty and I was being told I was not welcome there.

This tension always comes to mind when the media brings news of soldiers returning from overseas conflicts. At some point a voice of protest is heard from among the returning wounded and disfigured soldiers. On arrival they are routinely kept away from the press photographers. No sight of wounds is allowed to spoil the celebrations.

I have suggested that some Christian traditions can be trapped in a mistaken view of suffering that actually excludes the transforming power of resurrection life. But the hymns and songs of today's charismatic renewal movements in the Church, for all their vitality and vision, have yet to honour the wounds of the risen Lord. These wounds are needed to temper a disturbing enthusiasm for military language, for marching, winning victories and crushing evil.

The American preacher, Tony Campolo, made the same point in a different way when he warned that resurrection life (or 'life in the Spirit') 'is not about having wonderful spiritual experiences of joy and worship, or speaking in tongues, victorious praying, or seeing dramatic healings and visions (though they have their place). To be filled with the Spirit is to have your heart broken by the same things that broke Jesus's heart'.[5]

Ultimately there is no resurrection that is not a resurrection out of hell.

It is the mark of a mature community of resurrection that it can find room for the expression of pain and struggle without the death of hope – and enter the celebration of hope and victory without excluding or neglecting those who still suffer. 'Rejoice with those who rejoice,' wrote St Paul, 'weep with those who weep' (Romans 12.15).

It was in this spirit that Jean Vanier, founder of the L'Arche communities, suggested that every act of Christian celebration should include a time of silence to remember those who could not yet celebrate. In such a place Christ can come and reveal himself as companion in our wounds as well as calling us into celebration of his victory.

Without shame

The vision of a wounded and risen Christ on Easter Day invites us to live more honestly with the wounds we carry ourselves. Most of us choose not to if we can avoid it. John Goldingay has written very movingly of the experience of sharing life and ministry with his wife Ann, who suffers from multiple sclerosis.

When I go and speak at some conference, often the thing that people take away is not anything I have said but their meeting with Ann, though they rarely articulate what it is that has affected them. My guess is that she embodies human characteristics which belong to us all but which we normally seek to evade, such a fragility, dependence and uncertainty. She brings these demons out into the open in such a way as they cease to be demons. Indeed, she reveals that they are angels. They are part of being human, part of the nakedness which humanity originally wore without shame, and they are therefore part of imaging God.[6]

Reflecting on how her illness has influenced his own life (as a theological college principal) he says,

I know in my own person that the disabled exercise an important ministry to the ordinary. [I have] institutional power which I can misuse, I can beat students in an argument most of the time if I choose to do so. Imagine what a so-and-so I might have been if it were not for the positive shaping effect on me of Ann's disability. I know she slows me down, for good. She makes me appreciate simple things, like squirrels, clouds and the swaying of the willow tree outside our house.

Ann's illness frees both tears and frustration, both love and anger, both resilience and guilty powerlessness. God does not organize, dominate, or do miracles for Ann. God lets her be. Perhaps she ministers to God.[7]

Glorious scars

If there are no marks on the risen Jesus then resurrection is only for the unmarked. When we see him marked, we dare to celebrate that we may rise too.

The hope of resurrection is found precisely where life most contradicts it. Long before resurrection is concerned with any glorious ascent to the life of heaven, it will first *descend* and embrace our wounds. In fact there will be no resurrection without them. Our renewal and transfiguring will begin from the place of our deepest defeat and despair.

This is the only way of making sense of this appearance of Christ, with such love and purpose, to a broken community, hiding behind locked doors for fear of the outside world. In his wounds, they recognized their own.

The wounds of Jesus are very significant for our understanding of his ascension into heaven. In Luke's Gospel, where the ascension is the final resurrection appearance, Jesus 'lifted up his hands and blessed them' (Luke 24.51, NIV). These are the same scarred hands by which the disciples had earlier come to recognize him. He then ascends in the same glorified *and wounded* body.

For this reason Jesus has been described as 'the wounded man in the heavens',[8] bearing in his own body the needs and longings of this world before the Father's throne.

It is the most fearful hope of all that Christ calls us to rejoice in. That somewhere there is a place where our deepest struggles with loss and brokenness are held in an embrace that promises new life.

And Christ in his resurrection, with his glorious scars, is the pledge of our transfiguring too – wounds and all.

On Easter night, during the vigil of resurrection, there is an ancient symbolic ritual. Into the large Paschal Candle at the front of the church, the priest presses five grains of incense and says the words:

'By his holy and glorious wounds, may Christ our Lord guard us and keep us.'

8

The marks of believing
Jesus and Thomas

———

But Thomas (who was called the Twin), one of the twelve, was not with them when Jesus came. So the other disciples told him, 'We have seen the Lord.' But he said to them, 'Unless I see the mark of the nails in his hands, and put my finger in the mark of the nails and my hand in his side, I will not believe.'

A week later his disciples were again in the house, and Thomas was with them. Although the doors were shut, Jesus came and stood among them and said, 'Peace be with you.' Then he said to Thomas, 'Put your finger here and see my hands. Reach out your hand and put it in my side. Do not doubt but believe.' Thomas answered him, 'My Lord and my God!' Jesus said to him, 'Have you believed because you have seen me? Blessed are those who have not seen and yet have come to believe.'

(John 20.24–29)

Where was Thomas on the night that Jesus appeared to the disciples?

Was he taking an urgent phone call? Had he popped out to collect a take-away meal? Doors locked after him. Can we

94

imagine him returning with the food ('Five plaice and chips, seven cod and chips, two pasty and chips, three pancake rolls and a large bottle of Diet Coke') to find everyone so overwhelmed and excited that no one is interested in eating?

Wherever Thomas had gone that day he had left his friends behind locked doors, fearing the violence of the authorities and still deep in the trauma of the death of Jesus. He returned to find himself bombarded with astonishing stories of Jesus appearing to them. 'We have seen the Lord!'

How would you have felt? The shock must have been enormous.

Thomas is remembered for his doubts, but he might equally be remembered for his unfortunate lack of timing.

This is the man who managed to miss the resurrection!

True believer

We know very little about Thomas. Apart from this story he only makes two other appearances in the Gospels. We first meet him after Jesus had announced he was returning to an area where his life had only recently been seriously threatened. When the disciples failed to change his mind, Thomas turned to the others and said, 'Let us also go, that we may die with him' (John 11.16). Whether this was meant sarcastically or out of misplaced bravado we don't know. But he shows no understanding of what Jesus is saying or doing.

On another occasion Jesus was preparing his followers for his coming 'departure' (the word he sometimes used to speak of his approaching death). He tells them he is going to prepare a place for them. 'And you know the way to where I am going,' he says.

Thomas bluntly contradicts this assumption. 'Lord, we don't know where you are going, so how can we know the way?' He is as confused as ever, but his honesty (and cheek?) are rewarded as he draws from Jesus one of the most famous sayings he ever gave. 'I am the way, and the truth, and the life. No one comes to the Father except through me' (John 14.1–6).

Taken together, the three stories give us a picture of a down-to-earth character, capable of large enthusiasms and great stubbornness. He contributes no distinctive insights. Like his fellow disciples he is easily confused by what he sees and hears of Jesus. What stands out is his directness and honesty. He had a quality that the writer Graham Greene always looked for in what he liked to call 'true believers'. This was 'a certain capacity for disloyalty; a refusal to go along with the crowd or toe the line'. Greene believed this made a true believer incapable of committing atrocities. They are not the kind of people who would plead that they were 'just obeying orders'.[1]

Every community needs characters like Thomas. They are the people who are willing to ask the questions that no one else dares to. They are truthful and they keep their friends more truthful too.

Doubt and faith

It is important to recognize that in this resurrection story Thomas in some way represents all the disciples. The Gospels record that they *all* doubted the resurrection. Even at the very end of Matthew's Gospel, where Jesus met his 11 disciples on the mountain top and commissioned them with the gospel, we read, 'When they saw him, they worshipped him; but some doubted' [literally 'drew back'] (Matthew 28.17).

It is perhaps to illustrate something of their struggles to believe and trust in the risen Jesus that St John tells the story of one of them – Thomas. He intended the experience of Thomas to be a personal example of what they all wrestled with. The story is an encouragement and challenge to those who come after.

The prayer for St Thomas' Day recognizes this when it thanks God:

> . . . who, for the firmer foundation of *our* faith,
> allowed your holy apostle Thomas
> to doubt the resurrection of your Son,
> till word and sight convinced him . . . [my italic][2]

John began the story by reminding us that Thomas was a twin (the meaning of 'Didymus'). Whether he intended it or not, this has often been taken as a symbolic way of saying what this story is about – the relationship of doubt and faith in Christian life. They are twins.

If that is true, then it is evident that this story has been much misused. How did the Church come to rename this disciple as '*Doubting* Thomas'? No Gospel writer gave him that nickname. More to the point, it is not true. He believed.

No other disciple has such a name. We don't speak of 'Peter the *Denier*' or '*Promiscuous* Mary Magdalene'. So why has the Church persisted in naming this follower of Jesus as an unbeliever? What is it about doubting that the Christian community cannot forget or forgive?

True faith will have a lively, if not comfortable relationship with doubt. And doubt is only overcome by going through it. Doubts do not decompose if you bury them. But the popular Christian understanding of faith all too easily leaves us feeling that our doubts and questions are not acceptable. We must hide them. Doubt is seen as a lack of faith. It is the opposite of believing. The tragedy of such a faith, however sincerely held, is that it has nothing to give us when we most need help.

'I know I shouldn't doubt and I should have faith but I do find it hard to understand what has happened and why God allowed it.' The speaker was a woman who was struggling to cope with a series of personal tragedies in her life. Her understanding of faith was clear and very sad. Faith meant accepting whatever happened to us. It meant being polite and respectful to God. It meant not complaining and not asking questions. And so, in the midst of her pain, anger and bewilderment, she could not share her struggles with God as she really needed to.

I can remember a precise moment when I could stomach

that view no longer. I was sitting in a prayer meeting, called after a football stadium disaster in which a large number of people were crushed to death. The mood was subdued. No one knew what to say. This disaster seemed to be the latest in a succession of tragedies.

We bowed before God, weighed down with pain and unable to express it. A few prayers were offered but they felt pious and empty. We kept lapsing into silence. From the back a voice suddenly burst out, 'Lord, I just don't know what you're playing at. I don't know what you think you're doing. It's so hard to believe in you when things like this keep happening.'

Those words freed something in me. I went home and told God exactly what I thought of him. I told him of the pain and shame of trying to speak of him in a world where such things happened. I confessed my fear that my faith would not be strong enough to survive in a world like this.

Faith to doubt

I have since discovered that this kind of 'doubt' is held in very high esteem in the Bible. Living faith is marked by the willingness to question and even challenge God's ways. Doubting, questioning and even protesting are signs of a real relationship with God.

The people of the Old Testament spoke to God with breathtaking directness. Utterly perplexed by God's dealings with him, Moses cried out, 'Why do you treat your servant so badly? In what respect have I failed to win your favour, for you to lay the burden of all these people on me?' (Numbers 11.11–15, NJB). Many of the psalms address God with the same boldness. 'Answer me when I call, O God!' (Psalm 4.1, RSV). 'Lord, why have you rejected me? Why have you hidden your face from me? . . . My friend and my neighbour you have put away from me and darkness is my only companion' (Psalm 88.15, 19).

This is a core feature of Jewish faith. Abraham Heschel writes:

> The refusal to accept the harshness of God's ways in the name of his love was an authentic form of prayer. Indeed, the ancient Prophets of Israel were not in the habit of consenting to God's harsh judgment and did not simply nod, saying 'Thy will be done.' They often challenged him, as if to say, 'Thy will be changed.' They had often countered and even annulled divine decrees [. . .] A person who lived by honesty could not be expected to suppress their anxiety when tormented by profound perplexity. They had to speak out audaciously. Human beings should never capitulate, even to the Lord.[3]

Good doubt

The vitality and boldness of such relating to God is notably absent in much Christian spirituality. Our relationship to God is more often spoken of in terms of ever more refined submission. But the willingness to question and challenge

God is not a sign of rebellion but a sign of real faith. Submission may require no faith at all.

One of the challenges in leading any groups of Christians in discussion or prayer is to try to break through to a more real, immediate way of addressing each other and God. We are often too scared of 'getting it wrong' or assume that being a Christian means a certain kind of politeness that actually involves never saying or praying what is really on your heart or mind.

It can feel like quite a risk to take. But the discovery of how the freedom to question faith actually brings faith to life is so exciting. We sometimes speak of acting in 'good faith'. We also need the possibility of living with 'good doubt'. The truth is that human nature is most fulfilled when it is questing and questioning. We are made to be explorers and searchers. And when we think we have found the answers we grow dull and make our bed on them. I have long thought that Christian evangelism has over-emphasized Jesus as 'the answer' to life. I know what is meant by that statement. But the picture of faith as finding an answer easily implies that something is complete and finished. That has never been my experience. Rather, Christ is the one in whom all life suddenly becomes infinitely greater, more costly, more glorious – and wonderfully alive to its God. Someone once observed, 'God is the surprise of the universe, not the answer.'

This was certainly our experience in those discussion evenings. We sometimes stumbled home with more questions than we arrived with. We often struggled with confusion. Nor was everyone who came convinced. But we never lost the sense that God enjoyed those evenings too.

My Lord and my God

We do not know why Thomas doubted what his friends told him. Our doubts and questions are never simply intellectual issues. So many personal factors affect our freedom to trust, or need to question what we hear. Our whole experience of life – good and bad – is revealed in how we respond to new discoveries. In my experience one of the factors that most inhibits people when faced with the challenge of new experience of God, is the pain of having been let down before. Thomas may have been resentful that he had missed such a life-changing encounter. Spiritual jealousy is much more common than we admit. I have always been one of those frustrated people who seem to be among the few still standing up or *not* shaking at the end of dramatic charismatic meetings. And as I step over the bodies in the aisles and struggle past shaking prayer groups to reach the exit, feeling very left out, I wonder if this is what Thomas felt like.

But this whole story is actually a wonderful and unexpected encouragement to those who find it hard to believe the way everyone else seems to. There is hope here for those who don't seem to share the experience that everyone else seems to have had. There is a place for people who don't conform to the way the community of faith believes.

Jesus personally seeks out a doubter on the edge of the

faith. Not only that, he agrees to Thomas' demands to examine and probe his wounds.

But he brings to him a particular challenge. 'Stop doubting and believe.' The original Greek here expresses a fuller meaning. It could be translated 'Stop doubting *once and for all* and *keep on* believing.' Doubt, questioning and scepticism can become compulsive. Jesus is telling Thomas that he needs to come off the fence and commit himself one way or the other.

In the Bible, doubts and questions are never an excuse for avoiding commitment.

'I've got a lot of questions,' said one man I once visited. I was there (at his wife's invitation) to discuss the baptism of his baby boy. He was explaining why he didn't come to church. At least *he* seemed to think it was an explanation. He sat there with a large glass of whisky, a successful businessman in a comfortable house. In the hall was a large bag of golf clubs and in the drive was an expensive car. Nothing wrong with any of that of course. But he did not look like a man deeply troubled by questions. He didn't seem to lack sleep. He certainly hadn't lost his appetite.

Real questions leave their mark on us. They haunt, irritate and disturb us. They give us no rest. They force us to get more involved with life, not less. Our doubts remind us of our frailty and lack of understanding. They humble us.

This is where true faith emerges from. 'It is not as a boy that I believe in Christ,' wrote Fyodor Dostoevsky, 'but my hosanna has passed through a great furnace of doubts.'

Doubts are not an excuse for laziness.

Faith and sight

Strangely, the one place in this story where Thomas appears to be criticized is at the very moment he declares his faith. 'Because you have seen me, you have believed,' said Jesus; 'blessed are those who have not seen and yet have believed.' This is very good news for the Christian generations that followed the era of the first apostles and who never witnessed Christ in human flesh. It is an easy temptation to assume that believing must have been easier for people in the Gospels than it is for us. Jesus warns against making that mistake.

In fact it is clear that the sight of Jesus was never a guarantee of faith. Many people saw Jesus and were *not* convinced by him. One of the greatest paradoxes in the Gospels is the way that the 'ungodly', the 'sinners' recognized the Son of God, while the 'godly', 'religious' people were unable to see who was before them. It was a blind man who called out in faith and was healed, while Jesus warned the watching Pharisees, saying. 'If you were blind, you would not be guilty, but since you say "We can see", your guilt remains' (John 9.41, NJB).

Seeing is not believing. The decision to believe involves an act of faith, and so does the decision not to believe. The 'life of faith' is not something only religious people undertake. It is the only way we can live in this world. I met someone at a party once who, on discovering I was a Christian, told me he was an atheist. He said it with a finality that implied that we had nothing in common. 'So we are both believers,' I replied. He looked astonished and very disappointed.

Life itself requires constant acts of faith. I have no certainty that my car is perfectly safe before I drive it. I have no certain guarantee that the food I buy at the supermarket will not poison me. Everything I do requires a fundamental act of trust.

And the more significant my choices, the greater is the uncertainty involved. And if daily living requires such trust and risk, how much more will we struggle to commit ourselves to God?

For the poet R. S. Thomas, the journey of faith and prayer grows more vulnerable rather than less with the passing years:

> Young
> I pronounced you. Older
> I still do, but seldomer
> now, leaning far out
> over an immense depth, letting
> your name go and waiting,
> somewhere between faith and doubt,
> for echoes of its arrival.[4]

Leap of faith

After taking everything into account, after checking and rechecking and taking all possible advice, we are still left with no option.

We must risk committing ourselves – to 'stop doubting and believe' – or not.

Here is how one person described facing the risk of belief or unbelief:

There is a gap between the probable and the proved. How was I to cross it? If I were to stake my whole life on the risen Christ, I wanted proof. I wanted certainty. I wanted to see him eat a bit of fish. I wanted letters of fire across the sky. I got none of these . . . It was a question of whether I was to accept him – *or reject*. My God! There was a gap *behind* me as well! Perhaps the leap to acceptance was a horrifying gamble – but what of the leap to rejection? There might be no certainty that Christ was God – but, by God, there was no certainty that he was not. This was not to be borne. I could not reject Jesus. There was only one thing to do once I had seen the gap behind me. I turned away from it, and flung myself over the gap towards Jesus.[5]

9

The far side

The restoration of Peter

———➤•◦◄———

After these things Jesus showed himself again to the disciples by the Sea of Tiberias; and he showed himself in this way. Gathered there together were Simon Peter, Thomas called the Twin, Nathanael of Cana in Galilee, the sons of Zebedee, and two others of his disciples. Simon Peter said to them, 'I am going fishing.' They said to him, 'We will go with you.' They went out and got into the boat, but that night they caught nothing.

Just after daybreak, Jesus stood on the beach; but the disciples did not know that it was Jesus. Jesus said to them, 'Children, you have no fish, have you?' They answered him, 'No.' He said to them, 'Cast the net to the right side of the boat, and you will find some.' So they cast it, and now they were not able to haul it in because there were so many fish. That disciple whom Jesus loved said to Peter, 'It is the Lord!' When Simon Peter heard that it was the Lord, he put on some clothes, for he was naked, and jumped into the lake. But the other disciples came in the boat . . . Jesus came and took the bread and gave it to them, and did the same with the fish.

(John 21.1–8, 13)

The story of Peter appears as an afterthought in John's Gospel. He clearly intended to finish his Gospel at the end of the previous chapter. There he told of the discovery of the empty tomb; Jesus appearing to Mary and giving her a message for the disciples; Jesus revealing himself to the disciples and commissioning them in the Holy Spirit. Thomas' journey from doubt to faith in Christ acts as a final parable, and John concluded his Gospel with a final appeal to his readers – 'that you may come to believe that Jesus is the Messiah, the Son of God, and that through believing you may have life in his name' (John 20.31).

Some time later, chapter 21 was added by John, or by someone carefully following his style. The reason may well have been popular demand. 'You can't finish the Gospel without telling us what happened to Peter!'

After these things

The story begins. The scene has changed from chapter 20. We do not know how long after, but the upper room in Jerusalem is now the shore of the Sea of Tiberias (the other name for Galilee). Now the same disciples who had been joyful in the resurrection a few verses before appear to be standing around wondering what to do next.

After the previous chapter we might be expecting some signs of new life and confidence among them. But the impression is one of drifting and restlessness.

Peter, as usual, takes the lead. He had more reason than

most to want to leave recent events behind. 'I'm going fishing,' he says. And the others all join him.

It is a poignant moment. For three years they had followed an extraordinary man they had come to believe was God. They had left everything for him. Now their lives had apparently gone full circle. The story was over for them. The most natural instinct, in times of insecurity, is to go back to a place that feels familiar and secure. They were going back to fishing.

They caught nothing all night.

The story is telling us something important here. It seems that not only are the disciples unable to enter new, risen life, they can find no way to re-enter their old life either. This is their dilemma. They are caught between two worlds, at home in neither. The scene is set for the third resurrection appearance.[1]

The charcoal fire

It is dawn and in the early light the disciples see a man standing on the shore. They are forced to admit to him that their nets are empty. He tells them to fish from the other side and suddenly their boat is almost sinking from the weight of fish.

In that moment Jesus is recognized.

Peter impulsively leaps out of the boat to swim for the shore – but not before getting dressed first! Most people take their clothes *off* before swimming. His need to cover himself before meeting Jesus is very revealing.

There on the shore is a charcoal fire.

The parallel is surely intentional. Only a few days before, in the chill and half light of early dawn, Peter had stood by a similar charcoal fire and been asked if he was a follower of Jesus.[2] There he had denied it three times.

The disciples must have felt very awkward. Jesus had caught them deserting. Peter's actions throughout betray a man desperate to please.

Jesus, however, appears completely relaxed. He greets them from the shore like a friendly hopeful customer – 'Haven't caught any fish, have you?' He then makes a gift of a miracle of fish so extravagant that it echoes his first miracle of wine at Cana (where Nathanael, among the group, came from).

When they stumble ashore he offers them breakfast and serves them. It must have been a strange meal. I can imagine the disciples sitting tongue-tied and embarrassed, forcing themselves to eat out of politeness.

But Jesus is described taking and giving bread and fish in phrases that would have deliberately reminded the disciples of both the Last Supper and also the wild generosity of the feeding of the 5,000.

The story moves on

When they had finished breakfast, Jesus said to Simon Peter, 'Simon son of John, do you love me more than these?' He said to him, 'Yes, Lord; you know that I love you.' Jesus said to him, 'Feed my lambs.' A second time

he said to him, 'Simon son of John, do you love me?'
He said to him, 'Yes, Lord; you know that I love you.'
Jesus said to him, 'Tend my sheep.' He said to him the
third time, 'Simon son of John, do you love me?' Peter
felt hurt because he said to him the third time, 'Do you
love me?' And he said to him, 'Lord, you know everything; you know that I love you.' Jesus said to him,
'Feed my sheep. Very truly, I tell you, when you were
younger, you used to fasten your own belt and to go
wherever you wished. But when you grow old, you will
stretch out your hands, and someone else will fasten a
belt around you and take you where you do not wish
to go.'

(John 21.15–18)

The story now focuses on one person. To be reconciled to
the risen Jesus will be something all the disciples must
struggle with. But this is Peter's story. The other disciples
withdraw and Peter is alone with Jesus.

What was it like? So much had painfully come between
them. Could Peter have ever expected Jesus to speak to him
again after what he had done?

In Mark's resurrection account the angels give the
women a message from Jesus for 'his disciples *and Peter*'
telling them they will meet him in Galilee (Mark 16.7). We
can only imagine what that personal note must have meant
to Peter. But as Mark records that the women fled in terror
and told no one, it may have been some time before Peter
got the message at all.

By the charcoal fire, Peter is once again questioned three times about his allegiance to Jesus. Twice he replies defensively, 'You know I love you!' Is he really surprised that Jesus should have to ask?

The third time finally cuts through to him. He is hurt and he surely knows why. But he still has no way of admitting his need or confessing his betrayal. He still pleads in self-justification, 'You *know* that I love you.' He wants to be able to repair the damage and move on without having to go back and face what he actually did. Between the lines he is really pleading, 'Can't we just forget about what happened and start afresh?'

Re-membering

Peter has a difficult and painful journey to make. He will not be able to enter new life until he has first returned to what still lies buried and unreconciled in his past. Lovingly but firmly that is where the repeated questions of Jesus lead him. There is no other way. 'Salvation does not bypass the history and memory of guilt, rather it builds upon it and from it.'[3]

Until there is a remembering, there can be no forgiveness. To re-member means to put something back together that has been broken and dis-connected. This means more than recalling an event or action from the past. It is not a feat of memory. The opposite of remembering is not forgetting. It is *dis*-membering.

To truly remember requires that we turn back to past

actions or relationships and recognize our place within what happened – perhaps for the first time. Only there can reconciliation be offered and received. There can be no healing or restoration 'until the memory itself is exposed, and exposed as a wound, a loss. The word of forgiveness is not audible for the one who has not "turned" to his or her past.'[4]

There is nothing more painful than a relationship so broken by mistrust or pain that even gestures of reconciliation and caring are interpreted as further evidence of treachery and it just makes matters worse. For a relationship to be restored there must be a willingness to turn to one another, and that always means facing our place in the cause of the pain. Anyone who has struggled to 'get it right' in seeking a reconciliation where the anger and wounds are deep knows the risk that Jesus took with Peter. Peter could so easily have refused to face it at all. He could have lost his temper and walked away.

Dis-membering

None of this will come as any surprise to those whose work is to minister in places of wounding and pain. The need for understanding and healing of memories, to be reconciled to people, events and hurts there, remains one of the most commonly expressed needs. It is also vividly illustrated through the experience of asylum seekers and victims of abuse or torture in our time. Before they can embrace any kind of new life they must find a way of recovering their past from the horrors they have endured. What is not remembered cannot be healed.

Do we ever really leave our past behind? Human beings live in and from history. The best listeners learn to be careful historians.

Watching the painstaking and harrowing work of searching mass graves in Kosovo, Iraq, Rwanda (and so many other places in these violent times) is to witness to the deep need to recover and truly name those people and events before life can hope to move on. The Truth and Reconciliation Commission in post-apartheid South Africa will long remain a particularly brave and inspirational example of this task.

Participation

An American friend speaks of the long struggle in her society to come to terms with the Vietnam war – a struggle reawakened again by the continued conflict in Iraq. She told of the overwhelming temptation to hide from the disaster that it became, by stressing the heroism, sacrifice and moral ideals of those who fought there. This is what made the Vietnam Memorial in Washington DC so significant. Its design was very controversial. When I visited it I could understand why. It was unlike any memorial I had ever seen before. Traditional war memorials *uplift* the names and memory of those who died. This tendency is stronger in Britain where war memorials are usually also monuments to victory. Memory is not therefore readily associated with being the victim or the overcome.

The Vietnam memorial is not a monument at all. You don't look up, you look down. You do not stand before it, still and silent – you enter it and participate. A path has been cut into the side of a small hill. It slopes gently down and up again alongside a wall of black marble on which the names of the dead and missing are engraved in endless columns. I watched two young women trace a name from the wall – perhaps a relative. A man was seen weeping and beating his fists against the wall in his grief. By inviting participation it both confronted and healed. It was a place to re-member.

I found the experience overwhelming. Unlike traditional memorials there was no separation between those who died and those who now remembered. There was no separation from the wounds of death and its meaning. Even as a foreigner, with no personal experience of war, I found myself led down into the dark wounds of recent history. There was no safe distance from which to observe and stay safely detached. By inviting participation it was a place that both confronted and healed.

Returning

Memory alone cannot save us. It may just as easily break or overwhelm us. If there are some who can shut out all remembrance there are many who long to forget and cannot. 'Fifty years – and I've never left the place,' wept a Jewish survivor on her recent return to Auschwitz.

True remembrance and reconciliation is costly. And we

must journey towards it without any certainty of the outcome. So there should be a caution in telling the more dramatic 'breakthrough' stories.

I recall hearing a speaker on the subject of the healing of memories telling of the deep bitterness he carried because of his treatment as a child by his parents. Simply and undramatically he told how, for the last 30 years, he had daily prayed words of forgiveness for his parents and sought the love, mercy and healing of Christ for those memories of childhood and home.

For some, the moment of release and healing may be quite sudden. For many others, the task of re-membering remains painful, costly and requires patient compassion – like tending a deep wound that is slow to heal and needs regular rebinding and cleansing. This is why there is a need in Christian worship for words of penitence, forgiveness and absolution. We need to receive again the cleansing of our wounded nature and to hear again of the promise of final healing.

In the light of all this we begin to recognize the compassion with which Jesus ministers to Peter. Jesus accompanies Peter back into the memory of his most terrible failure and betrayal, and so into his deepest self. There, by the charcoal fire, he waits to meet him again, for only there can Peter be forgiven and restored. The most loving gift Jesus can offer him is to lead him to the place where he faces his true self, and be there himself when he arrives. Perhaps the primary ministry of the risen Jesus is precisely this – to give us back our memories. What we forget, leave behind, deny or simply cannot face by ourselves, he holds in living remembrance until we can come to a place where we can receive it back.

What Christ did for Peter he constantly works to do for us.

The wound of love

Peter's deepest encounter in this story was not with himself, his awfulness, sin and guilt. It was with divine love. It was love that sought him, not judgement. Love had led him to this place. With love, Jesus now commissioned him in service again. 'On the far side of resurrection, vocation and forgiveness occur together, always and inseparably.'[5] The real burden of Christ's forgiveness is that it leaves us struggling with the knowledge that we are loved without condition. Although it is the news we most long to hear, nothing in our lives ever quite prepares us for this place, and the reality is frightening to us. Not surprisingly, someone once called the experience of forgiveness the 'hell of mercy'.

Like Peter, when we come to the place of our true memory, of our sins and capacity for darkness, our greatest struggle will not be with sin, evil or judgement. It will be with goodness, with mercy, with the terrifying and joyful wonder of being loved by God.

In *The Lord of the Rings*, the Company of the Ring have narrowly avoided disaster and have been resting in the healing enchantment of beauty of the woods of Lorien, in the care of the beautiful Elf Queen. All too soon, the time comes to resume the journey. As they leave, Gimli the Dwarf weeps his grief at leaving such a place of love and healing. 'Why did I come on this Quest? Little did I know where the chief peril lay! Torment in the dark was the danger that I feared, and it did not hold me back. But I would not have come, had I known the danger of light and joy. Now I have taken my worst wound in this parting. Alas!'[6]

'To have opted for love', wrote Brother Roger of Taizé, 'is to open yourself to a wound from which you never recover.'

> God of terror and joy,
> you arise to shake the earth.
> Open our graves
> and give us back the past;
> so that all that has been buried
> may be freed and forgiven,
> and our lives may return to you
> through the risen Christ, Amen.[7]

10

What is that to you?

A postscript

━━━➤●◄━━━

'Why do you look for the living among the dead?'

(Luke 24.5)

We do not come to this new, risen life naturally. If we did we would have found it long ago. It is a gift from Jesus, who of his own free, unfathomable choice, desires to seek us out and bring us home. Our story begins and ends with him.

The great encouragement of the first resurrection community was that it was made up of such an unpromising group of people. None of them came to it naturally. They were grief-stricken, fearful, theologically confused, full of doubts and prejudices, locked away from the world, or planning to return to their old way of life. And that is where Jesus came and met each of them. Each encounter, each word and action, lovingly fitted to the one before him.

The good news lies in this very contradiction. This is the work of the risen Christ. And if he so carefully and patiently pursues such improbable people, he surely seeks us too.

Between the momentous cosmic events of Easter, Ascension and Pentecost, these brief, unexpected stories of the resurrection appearances give us hope where we would not otherwise dare to look for it. For it is here that we find ourselves too: somewhere between death and resurrection, seeking the dead yet puzzling over rumours of life. And this is where Jesus will find us, and our remaking will be just as improbable and unexpected.

High up in the archway of a north entrance to Chartres Cathedral is a carving called 'The Creation of Adam'.[1] God is sitting beside the figure of Adam, who has emerged as far as his waist out of the dust of the earth. Adam is leaning against God, resting his head on his lap, his right hand clutching God's knee. He looks exhausted with the effort of being created. Perhaps he is asleep. Perhaps he has yet to receive breath at all.

With his right hand, God supports Adam's head, while his left hand is poised over him as if about to stroke his hair. They could be the hands of a potter over a clay. But when I showed a photograph of this sculpture to a group, one of the participants was a midwife. She insisted that the hands of God were poised in exactly the right professional position a midwife takes up as the baby's head appears and begins the turn that enables the rest of the body to follow. God as our midwife – knowing what it takes. Knowing when to urge us to push or to rest.

Knowing when to push and when to rest is a vital insight in the manic urgency of our times. The sculptor of Chartres seems to have frozen the action at a resting place in creation.

Do you find it easy to think of God *in*active at all? Do not our times and our Church need something altogether more urgent and decisive? Taking questions at a conference on mission, a speaker was presented with the familiar fact that while the Church is growing faster around the world than ever, it is in serious decline in Western Europe. He was asked to comment on this. The answer is usually to tell Westerners we must 'push harder'. 'Well,' he said, gently, 'we just don't know how it looks to God.'

Chartres Cathedral is nearly 800 years old. Beneath those soaring arches have flowed centuries of wars, plagues, prosperity, poverty, faith, apostasy, hope, despair, laughter and tears.

And where has God been during this time? He's over there, high above that side entrance. If you didn't know where to look, you would easily miss him.

His head is upright. His eyes (perhaps from the effect of centuries of weathering) appear closed. The mood is of intense care and concentration – quiet, attentive, unhurried. Look at those hands. They seem to have been poised there for ever. What is he waiting for? There is no apparent urgency to finish the job.

So God creates with the ease and passion of one for whom such work is life itself. There is no hurry. He has all eternity.

But nothing will distract him from completing what he has begun.

As I gaze on the sculpture I want to ask a question. It is always the same one: 'How long does it take – all this becoming, this strange elusive life of yours?'

The answer is always the same. (And always the hint of a smile behind that stone face.)

'As long as you like.'

Notes

Introduction

1 Quoted in Pauline Warner, *Women's Icons of Ministry*, Cambridge: Grove Books 1994, p. 11.

2 For a full and accessible theological study of this whole subject see N. T. Wright, *The Resurrection of the Son of God*, London: SPCK 2003.

3 N. T. Wright, *The Resurrection of the Son of God*, part 4, section 13.

4, 5 Both phrases from a passage of C. S. Lewis's comment on the writing of Charles Williams. In the context of the chapters that follow, the passage is worth quoting in full:

> Christians naturally think more often of what the world has inflicted on the saints; but the saints also inflict much on the world. Mixed with the cry of martyrs, the cry of nature wounded by Grace, also ascends – and presumably to heaven . . . [Williams] had no belief in a conception of Grace which simply abolishes nature; and he felt that there was always something legitimate in the protests of nature against the harrowing operation of conversion.

Quoted in Simon Tugwell, *Reflections on the Beatitudes*, London: DLT 1980, p. 67.

Notes

1 A door has cracked open

1 Philip Seddon, *Darkness*, Cambridge: Grove Books 1983, p. 3.
2 From the Third Eucharistic Prayer, *Alternative Service Book*, London, Clowes, Cambridge: SPCK 1980, p. 137.
3 Stephen Davis, *Risen Indeed: Making Sense of the Resurrection*, London: SPCK 1994, p. 184.
4 This belief has found popular expression in the meditation 'Death is nothing at all' by Canon Henry Scott Holland and is often requested as a reading at funeral services.

> Death is nothing at all . . . I have only slipped away into the next room. I am I and you are you. Whatever we were to each other that we are still. Call me by my old familiar name, speak to me in the easy way which you always used. Put no difference in your tone; wear no forced air of solemnity or sorrow. Laugh as we always laughed at the little jokes we enjoyed together. Play, smile, think of me, pray for me. Let it be spoken without effort, without the ghost of a shadow on it. Life means all it ever meant. It is the same as it ever was; there is absolute unbroken continuity. What should I be out of mind because I am out of sight? I am waiting for you for an interval, somewhere very near, just around the corner. All is well.

Quoted in James Bentley, Andrew Best and Jackie Hunt (eds), *Funerals: A Guide*, Hodder & Stoughton 1994, No. 425. The irony is that he wrote this as an illustration of a popular but mistaken view of death. It represents a serious distortion of Christian understanding of death and afterlife. Far from treating death as an 'insignificant' or 'negligible accident' to be brushed aside, Jesus faced it as an enemy. He confronted it, descended into the hell of it and defeated it in his own body.

5 Stephen Davis, *Risen Indeed*, p. 30.
6 Tom Stoppard, *Arcadia*, London: Faber and Faber 1993, pp. 47–8.
7 Michael Bourdeaux, *Risen Indeed: Lessons in Faith from the USSR*, London: DLT 1983, pp. 41–2.
8 The story is told in Mary Craig, *Candles in the Dark: Six Modern Martyrs*, London: Hodder & Stoughton 1984, p. 164.
9 Stephen Davis, *Risen Indeed*, p. 10.

10 Charles Handy, *The Age of Unreason*, London: Random House Publishers 1995, p. 4ff.

11 The meditation is my own.

2 Loving the space between

1 Metropolitan Anthony Bloom, *School for Prayer*, London: DLT 1989, chapter 1.

2 Nico Kazantzakis, *Zorba the Greek*, London: Faber 1980, p. 125.

3 I wrote more fully about aspects of this time in *Space for God*, London: DLT 1990.

4 Quoted in Alan Jones, *Soul Making*, London: SCM 1986, p. 122.

5 Kahlil Gibran, *The Prophet*, London: Pan 1982, p. 16. He is writing about marriage.

6 Quoted in a personal letter from a friend. Original source unknown.

7 Quoted in Andrew Louth, *The Wilderness of God*, London: DLT 1991, p. 151.

3 Why are you weeping?

1 For a rare and profound theological reflection on tears see Maggie Ross, *The Fountain and the Furnace: The Way of Tears and Fire*, New Jersey: Paulist Press 1987, p. 243ff.

2 Notable exceptions are Alan Jones, *Soul Making*, London: SCM 1986, chapter 4 and Richard Foster, *Prayer*, San Francisco: HarperCollins 2003, chapter 4.

3 Maggie Ross, *The Fountain and the Furnace*, p. 238.

4 Maggie Ross, *The Fountain and the Furnace*, p. 10.

5 Maggie Ross, *The Fountain and the Furnace*, p. 138.

6 By an unknown monk of the thirteenth century. Quoted in André Louf, *Teach us to Pray*, London: DLT 1978, p. 38.

7 Maggie Ross, *The Fountain and the Furnace*, p. 14.

8 J. R. R. Tolkien, *The Lord of the Rings*, London: Unwin 1978, p. 990.

4 Stranger on the road

1 Mark Stibbe, *John's Gospel (New Testament Readings)*, Oxford: Routledge 1994, pp. 13–14.

2 Walter Brueggemann, *Hopeful Imagination: Prophetic Voices in Exile*, London: SCM 1986, p. 71.

3   Rowan Williams, *Ponder These Things*, Norwich: Canterbury Press 2002, p. 50.
4   Described in David Runcorn, *Space for God*, London: DLT 1990, pp. 68–9.
5   Erich Fromm, quoted in Kenneth Leech, *True God*, London: Sheldon Press 1985, p. 183.
6   Kenneth Leech, *The Eye of the Storm: Living Spiritually in a Real World*, San Francisco: HarperCollins 1992, p. 221.
7   Rowan Williams, *Open to Judgment: Sermons and Addresses*, London: DLT 1994, pp. 158–9.
8   A. J. Malherbe and E. Ferguson (trans.), *Life of Moses* (Classics of Western Spirituality), New Jersey: Paulist Press 1978, pp. 115–16.

5 Some of our women amazed us

1   Quoted in Charles Elliott, *Praying the Kingdom*, London: DLT 1985, p. 32.
2   Discussed in Kenneth Bailey, 'Women in the New Testament: A Middle Eastern Cultural View' in *Anvil*, Vol. 11, No. 1, 1994, pp. 11–12.
3   Kenneth Bailey, 'Women in the New Testament: A Middle Eastern Cultural View' in *Anvil*, Vol. 11, No. 1, 1994, p. 15ff. Bailey is very helpful in understanding the significance of the cultural context of the New Testament and how it influenced Paul's teaching about women.
4   Amartya Sen, 'More Than 100 Million Women Are Missing' in *New York Review of Books* (12/20/90), pp. 61–6. There is no shortage of discussion of this study on the internet. See <http://ucatlas.ucsc.edu/gender/gender_mortality.php> for a useful summary of the study and related issues.
5   Alan Ecclestone, *Scaffolding of the Spirit*, London: DLT 1987, p. 64.
6   *Common Worship Initiation Services*, London: Church House Publishing 2000.
7   Janet Martin Soskice, in Andrew Walker (ed.), *Different Gospels*, London: SPCK 1993, pp. 198–9.

6 This is flesh I'm talking about here!

1 James Morrow, *Towing Jehovah*, London: Granada 1994.

2 Etty Hillesum, *An Interrupted Life*, London: Persephone Books 1999, p. 42. I explore this more fully in *Spirituality Workbook: A Guide for Explorers, Pilgrims and Seekers*, London: SPCK 2006, chapter 11.

3 James Nelson, *The Intimate Connection*, London: SPCK 1992, p. 23.

4 The word which medieval theologians used to describe the special abilities of Jesus' resurrection body.

5 Quoted in Raymond Brown, *The Gospel According to John*: Vol. 2 XIII–XXI, London: Geoffrey Chapman 1972, p. 990.

6 C. S. Lewis develops this idea in his fantasy *The Great Divorce*, London: Fount 2002.

7 Rubem Alves, *I Believe in the Resurrection of the Body*, Philadelphia: Fortress Press 1984, pp. 7–8.

8 Rubem Alves, *I Believe in the Resurrection of the Body*, p. 9.

9 Toni Morrison, *Beloved*, London: Vintage 1997, pp. 88–9. I have also drawn on an article on Toni Morrison by Mandy Russell-Jones in *Leading Light*, journal of the C. S. Lewis Centre, Vol. 1 (3 March 1994).

7 The wounds that keep us

1 For a more extended discussion of this issue see Tom Smail's very helpful contribution in Andrew Walker, Nigel Wright and Tom Smail, *Charismatic Renewal: The Search for a Theology*, London: SPCK 1993, part 2, chapter 4 ,'The Cross and the Spirit: Towards a Theology of Renewal'.

2 Thomas Kelly, in *Mission Praise*, New York: HarperCollins 2005, No. 647.

3 'Lo! He comes with clouds descending' in *Mission Praise*, New York: HarperCollins 2005, No. 424.

4 The order for the visitation of the sick in the Book of Common Prayer, Cambridge: Cambridge University Press 1964, p. 312.

5 Transcribed from a taped address.

6 Quoted by kind permission from *St John's Theological College*

Newsletter, No. 61 (December 1993). Goldingay reflects further on this theme in a subsequent newsletter, No. 65 (April 1995).
7   *St John's Theological College Newsletter.*
8   Bishop Simon Barrington-Ward, in conversation.

8 The marks of believing
1   Quoted from Alan Jones, *Soul Making*, London: SCM 1986, pp. 118–19.
2   *Common Worship*, London: Church House Publishing 2000, p. 436.
3   Quoted in Henri Nouwen, *Genesee Diary*, London: DLT 1995, p. 142.
4   R. S. Thomas, 'Waiting', in *Later Poems 1972–1982*, London: Macmillan 1983, p. 111. Copyright Kunjana 2001.
5   Sheldon Vanauken, *A Severe Mercy*, London: Hodder & Stoughton 1977, p. 98.

9 The far side
1   I refer to John 21.14. John appears to be counting appearances to *groups* rather than *individuals* at this point.
2   The Greek word *anthrakian* (charcoal fire) is the same in both instances, and only appears in the Gospel on these two occasions.
3   Rowan Williams, *Resurrection*, London: DLT 1982, p. 34.
4   Rowan Williams, *Resurrection*, p. 21.
5   Rowan Williams, *Resurrection*, p. 35.
6   J. R. R. Tolkien, *The Lord of the Rings*, London: Unwin 1978, p. 399.
7. Collect for Easter Day in Janet Morley, *All Desires Known*, London: SPCK 2005, p. 14.

10 What is that to you?
1   See my *The Creation of Adam: Seven Guided Reflections from Genesis*, Cambridge: Grove Books 2001.